Long Rods—Light Lines

LONG RODS
LIGHT LINES

Some Thoughts on Flyfishing

DAVE SOUTHALL

Dave Southall

Coch-y-Bonddu Books
2023

Long Rods—Light Lines: Some Thoughts on Flyfishing
By Dave Southall

ISBN: 978-1-915714-03-9

2023 © Coch-y-Bonddu Books Ltd, Machynlleth

Text © 2023 Dave Southall

Coch-y-Bonddu Books Ltd,
Machynlleth,
Powys, SY20 8DG

01654 702837

www.anglebooks.com

Printed in Malta by Gutenberg Press

All rights reserved. No part of this publication may be reproduced, stored in a retrieval system, or transmitted, in any form or by any means, electronic, mechanical, photocopying, recording or otherwise, without the prior consent of the copyright holders.

I would like to dedicate this, my first book, to my parents, Rupert and Mary Southall, who nurtured in me a love for, and reverence of, the natural world. Also to Stuart Crofts, since without his extensive knowledge of aquatic entomology, and his encouragement, I would not have become involved with the Riverfly Partnership and would not have gained a fraction of the knowledge that I now have.

CONTENTS

INTRODUCTION   11

1. SOME THOUGHTS ON WATERCRAFT AND THE LOCATION OF FISH
    Marginal Success   19
    Fish Lies   25
    Stealth   36

2. SOME THOUGHTS ON TACTICS
    Presentation   45
    Drag   54
    Pocket-water Fishing   58
    Chalk Streams and Spring Creeks   66
    Coping with Drought   77
    Fishing in the Cold   83
    Persisting   90
    Trials with Tenkara   97
    Italian Style Casting   104
    Floatants   109
    The Washing Line Method on Rivers   113

    A Paternoster Rig for Nymphing on Rivers and Lakes   114
    Sight-fishing   117
    Streamers   122

3. SOME THOUGHTS ON FLY DESIGN
    Fly Colour   127
    Fly Size   133
    Extended Bodies   138
    Feather Bodies   141
    CdC   145
    "Anchor-Bodied" Flies   151
    Visibility   158
    Spiders   161

4. SOME THOUGHTS ON ENTOMOLOGY
    Winter and Midges   167
    Large Dark Olives   173
    Bibionid Flies   175
    Agapaetus Pupae   177
    Heptagenids   180
    Aphids   183
    Beetles   189
    Big Mayflies   192
    Ants   195
    Dance Flies   197
    Stoneflies   199
    Caddis Flies   207
    Tipulids / Craneflies   210

5. **SOME THOUGHTS ON CONSERVATION AND FISHERY MANAGEMENT**
   A Precious Resource   215
   Conservation Groups   221
   Biosecurity   227

IN CONCLUSION   231

INTRODUCTION

My first introduction to fishing in its broadest sense was when, as a six-year-old boy, my dad took me pond dipping. I was fascinated by the water boatmen, leeches, pond snails, sticklebacks and sundry other bugs and beasties we captured. Not long after I was given the top section of a broken greenheart rod, to the top ring of which I attached a length of cord, a float and a hook to gut, plus a few lead shot. With this and a loaf of bread I managed to catch the small rudd that lived under the branches of a willow tree that overhung a local pond. Aged nine, my dad's uncle bought me a 7 ft long hollow fibreglass spinning rod and a small centrepin reel, which further fuelled my obsession with fishing.

In my teens, Richard Walker was my angling hero and carp, tench and pike were my primary quarry. I did have a brief dabble with flyfishing, using an old, heavy, very soggy-actioned split cane rod and a parallel silk line. With this I'd expectantly swing a Butcher, or Teal Blue and Silver across the flow of any stream that was reputed to hold trout, but a distinct lack of success soon curtailed my enthusiasm. It was not until I went to study biology at York University that I once again took to flyfishing. The Yorkshire Rye and Driffield Canal, both of which held trout and good grayling were in easy reach on my motorbike. I built a rod from a Hardy's Fibatube blank (a 7 ft for a 4/5 line), bought a Hardy geared fly-reel and loaded it with a modern plastic fly-line. With help from the writings of Frank Sawyer, G E M Skues, Oliver Kite and Eric Horsfall Turner, I gleaned the basics of flyfishing and fly-tying. As a result, I started to catch both trout and grayling. In the early spring I'd usually fish with a team of three flies, a

The author 1969, Yorkshire, River Rye

weighted Shrimp on the point, a Partridge and Orange on the first dropper and a dry Greenwell's Glory on the top dropper. The latter was as much as an indicator as a fish catcher. As spring progressed into early summer I'd substitute a lighter Sawyer Pheasant Tail Nymph on the point and a Snipe and Purple on the first dropper. Once 1 June arrived (the start of the Yorkshire coarse fishing season, in those days) the fly-rod was generally put away.

In the early 1970s I got a job with the Ministry of Agriculture, Fisheries and Food as a research worker in their laboratory at Harpenden in Hertfordshire. Carp and pike were still my main interests. However, some friends and I cleaned out an old cress bed in the Lee valley and stocked it with 50 rainbow and 50 brown trout. These fish soon became very educated and provided interesting and challenging fishing. They taught me the effectiveness of fishing small buzzer pupae suspended under a dry-fly. I also had the occasional trip to reservoirs like Hanningfield and Pitsford, fishing nymphs and lures with eight-weight shooting heads and a rod I built from a coarse fishing blank. In addition, I still made a visit or two each year to the Yorkshire Rye after grayling on the fly. In 1974, I took up a teacher's training course at Cheltenham and

INTRODUCTION

managed a few sessions on a tiny Gloucestershire stream dry-fly fishing for dace and the occasional trout. In 1975 I moved back to East Yorkshire and resumed my flyfishing on the Rye and Driffield Canal.

By 1977 rock climbing and mountaineering had taken over my life and I didn't touch a fishing rod again till 1998 when a back injury, caused whilst mountain biking, prompted me to get the coarse fishing gear out in search of chub. It was then that I discovered that my mountain biking friend, Steve Donohue, was also a keen flyfisherman. After having several sessions with him for small stillwater rainbows he prompted me to join the Derwent Anglers' Club which has ten miles of the upper Derwent near Scarborough. As a "probationer" I was restricted to the top three miles of tree-shrouded river (really just a small stream) that thoroughly tested and honed my casting. I caught just under 400 trout and grayling that first season and was well and truly hooked again.

Since then I have had the good fortune to fish a wide range of waters in the UK, whilst each year I try to have at least one trip to more exotic locations and have flyfished for brown trout on the Suir system of southern Ireland; for trout and grayling on Slovenia's Rivers Soča, Tolminka, Baca, Sava Bohinjka and Unica; brown trout, brook trout and grayling on Austria's Muir, Torrener Ache, Mondsee Ache, Salzach, Gerlos River and Krimmler Ache, plus many smaller streams; grayling in the rivers and lakes of arctic Sweden; brown trout, rainbows, brook trout and cutthroat trout in Montana and Wyoming; small-mouth bass, brook trout, rainbows and brown trout in the Smoky Mountains of Tennessee and North Carolina; grayling and trout on Poland's River San; plus large-mouth bass and bluegills in the lakes and streams of Florida and the trout of New Zealand's South Island.

In doing all this I have had the great privilege to meet and befriend a host of wonderfully generous anglers who have always been free with their advice and invitations to fish their home waters. Many of these friends have been made through my membership of the Grayling Society, Salmon and Trout Conservation and the Wild Trout Trust, all of which I would recommend to all other flyfishers who value the conservation of these species. I should particularly like to thank the following people:

First and foremost, my father and mother, who fostered in me a deep interest in the natural world, and who allowed me, and encouraged me, to go out into the countryside, often unsupervised, to explore its riches. In my opinion many parents nowadays have a far too exaggerated perception of the dangers in life and so are overprotective of their children. Mine I feel had the correct balance, allowing me to fish the local farm ponds and bug-hunt on my own. They also ensured that I had a good education, despite my natural laziness; without their persistent encouragement I would probably never have become a scientist and may well not have had the enquiring mind needed to become a successful angler.

Steve Donohue, who got me back into flyfishing and who has been a regular waterside companion of mine for over twenty years. I have learned a lot from our many discussions.

Stuart Crofts who I got to know through collecting adult caddis for his National Survey of Caddis, for which he is internationally famous, as well as having been captain of the English Rivers Flyfishing Team. A more knowledgeable yet unpretentiously genuine person one could not hope to meet. I have learned much from him, not least the importance of *Agapetus* pupae as trout and grayling food.

Mike Kendall who took up flyfishing at the age of thirteen, after I had been teaching his class about the aquatic food chains in the Driffield Canal. I showed them photos of the invertebrates and my fly-box of imitations, making the point that by flyfishing I was the top of the food chain. With his parents' permission he regularly joined me on my flyfishing trips. It was amazing how quickly he learned the required skills of fishing and fly-tying and I learned a lot whilst being his mentor. It always amazes me how unfettered the young are by the preconceptions and misconceptions of accepted wisdom.

INTRODUCTION

Rod Calbrade who published my first ever article in the *Grayling Society Journal*.

Mark Bowler who published my first articles in *Fly Fishing and Fly Tying* magazine. This book is based around some of that material.

Robin Goldthorpe of the East Yorkshire Branch of the Fly Dressers' Guild, who by asking me what I knew about Tenkara in the autumn of 2010 (which was virtually zero at the time) revolutionised my pocket-water fishing.

Emanuele Gonetto, a good fishing friend, who introduced me to the Italian style of casting, an amazing way of limiting drag on rivers with complex flows.

David Percival, river-keeper on the Cressbrook and Litton waters of the Derbyshire Wye, for his friendship and humour, plus giving me the chance to fish this stunning river.

Tom Bell of Sunray Fly Fish who introduced me to his Micro Thin, delicate presentation lines and his light-line long rods and who gave me the opportunity to write a regular blog on his website.

Tony Walsh, who, as well as being a great fishing companion, was one of the people who encouraged me to write this book.

Don Stazicker, Peter Hayes and Stuart Crofts for proof-reading the final draft of this book.

There are many others to whom I'm indebted for their kindness and friendship. I heartily apologise to them for not mentioning them individually.

MY FLYFISHING PHILOSOPHY

Not for me the mindless stripping of blobs and other sundry bits of Christmas tinsel, or the trolling of big lures behind a boat with an eight-weight rod for monster trout, although I would not condemn anyone for using any legitimate method of fishing. As a trained ecologist, and keen entomologist, imitative fishing is what fascinates me, plus the finesse of presenting a fly delicately and precisely in such a way that it behaves like the real thing. The achievement of good presentation is an obsession of mine, as is the design and selection of fly-patterns that can be presented appropriately and that have the requisite triggers to tempt a fish to take. As a result, my favourite fishing is dry-fly or sight fishing with nymphs using light lines and the longest rod practicable for the situation.

I am also an avid supporter of catch-and-release carried out in such a way that the fish are unharmed. With the high level of angling pressure on most fisheries, wild populations of trout and grayling are unable to sustain the regular removal of the best fish. These are not only the breeding stock, but also carry the genes for fast growth and in my view are too valuable to be killed. Stocking for me is an anathema. Stocked fish-farm fish rarely survive long in most fisheries, since they are often inbred and uneducated: they are poor competitors with the wild fish and are more vulnerable to predators. Furthermore, since they associate people and splashes with food, careless wading and casting may actually attract them. In addition, they are a potential source of disease and alien species may be transferred with them as they are transported from one river to another. I do, however, realise that in the real world, with pollution incidents and cormorant predation, stocking is sometimes necessary on some waters. In my opinion, river-fishery managers and clubs should strive to provide the correct habitat and policies to ensure self-sustaining populations of fish. To this end, at the time of writing, I am a trustee of the East Yorkshire Rivers Trust and local coordinator of data for the Riverfly Partnership Scheme, a body within which anglers and other volunteers monitor the invertebrates in their local rivers to keep an eye on the water quality.

THE AIM OF THIS BOOK

This book is not aimed at the raw beginner. It is targeted at those who have grasped the basics but wish to gain further insight into the entomological and presentational aspects of flyfishing, which can not only improve their catches

INTRODUCTION

but also enhance their understanding and enjoyment of this fascinating pastime. The great thing about it is that no matter how much one knows there will always be more to learn. Each chapter contains my thoughts on various aspects of our sport. Do not take what I say as gospel truth since I am as fallible as the next person, but think about what I've written and make up your own mind as to whether I was right or wrong.

I also aim to impress on the reader how important conservation and good river management are if we are to have good quality fishing with self-sustaining stocks of wild fish, rather than rivers full of tame, fish-farmed, stocked trout with ragged fins and a short life expectancy.

In my opinion the main requirements for consistent success as a flyfisher are an enquiring and open mind, an observant nature, plus a willingness to learn. It is an oft-quoted fact that 90 per cent of the fish are caught by 10 per cent of the anglers. Some readers may well be part of that 10 per cent, whilst hopefully the others will in time become a part of that small band of successful flyfishers. I trust that, whatever your skill level, you will find something to stimulate your grey cells in my ramblings, some of which have been previously published in *Fly Fishing & Fly Tying* magazine, the Sunray Fly Fish website blogs and the *Grayling Society Journal*, whilst others are new.

Although I have tried to put my thoughts into a logical sequence, each section/thought is a self-contained unit. As a result, there is inevitably some repetition, but I have attempted to keep this to a minimum.

1

SOME THOUGHTS ON WATERCRAFT AND THE LOCATION OF FISH

The flyfisher's first objective must be the location of his or her quarry. To achieve this objective we must think like a trout, grayling or whatever species we are targeting. What rivers or lakes hold them? Where within these waters are feeding fish likely to be located? Sometimes we may be lucky enough to see the fish, but often it may be necessary to search for them. Once the fish are located our next task is to avoid scaring them away.

MARGINAL SUCCESS

"Fish fine and far off to avoid scaring the fish…" is what I was always told during my early years of angling, in the 1960s. I'd go to my local carp lake kitted out with 12 ft long fast-taper rods plus overloaded fixed-spool reels and I'd cast my baits as close to infinity as possible. Alternatively, I'd visit one of the Midlands reservoirs with my 9 ft eight-weight rod, plus shooting head, where I'd double-haul my flies into the wide blue yonder. That's where the fish had to be, away from any bankside disturbance. I was young, naïve and impressionable in those long-past days. Distance casting was macho and a measure of the angler's skill. It did not strike me as odd that my success was inconsistent, with all too frequent blanks. It

Casting deep under the bankside trees, River Annan

took me a long time to realise that carp and trout (particularly brown trout) love the zone within a metre or two of the lake edge or riverbank.

Why do the margins hold such an attraction for the fish? The trout's two main requirements are shelter from predators and an easily accessible food source. The first is provided by overhanging trees and other vegetation, submerged roots of marginal trees, steep undercut banks, marginal drop-offs, weed-beds and reed beds. The second is available thanks to the supply of terrestrials that drop in or blow in from the banks to augment the aquatic food supply. The gut contents of trout often show a preponderance of terrestrials: beetles, caterpillars, centipedes, aphids, ants, grasshoppers, black gnats, hawthorn flies, heather flies, daddy-long-legs, slugs, worms and a host of others. Most of them are more likely to be found close to the margins. On windy days aquatic emergers, such as olives, midges and sedges/caddis flies, may also be blown to the windward edges of the stream or lake where there can be significant accumulations concentrated tight against the banks. Find such a spot during a hatch and superb sport is virtually assured.

On one of my local small stillwaters, I only fish if there is a strong west or north-west wind blowing. The other anglers think I'm mad when they see me head for one of the bays at the windward end of the lake and then commence fishing into the gale, particularly since I'm using a five-weight set-up. It's not a problem since I'm usually only casting a few yards along the bank to fish that are mopping up midges (adults and pupae) and other insect life, which has been trapped against the reeds. On large waters, strong onshore winds can create big waves which stir up invertebrates from the lake bed; it's surprising how many fish may be patrolling the edges of the disturbed, often coloured-up waters along the shoreline. Fish may not be intelligent but they can certainly learn where the best source of food is to be found. I, too, have learned not to ignore the bankside banquet with its attendant trout.

Sadly, many of the anglers I see seem to be unaware of this and so make little attempt to approach the lake, reservoir, or river with caution and stealth. The rainbows are spooked into the centre of the lake whilst the brownies bolt into the nearest safe place to sulk for a while. The only significant exception to this scenario is when the water has just been stocked with naïve stew-fed trout, which for a while, until they have learned better (if given the chance), will actually be attracted to anglers. These fish have been conditioned all their lives to associate people with food. Furthermore, they also associate any splash with food being thrown in to the stock pond, so careless casting may actually attract them by triggering the conditioned food-search reflex. Unfortunately, the regular, often heavy, stocking of many waters ensures that there are always enough "easy fish" to satisfy the undiscerning angler thus ensuring that some anglers never get the stimulus to progress beyond stockie-bashing. Now don't get me wrong; easy heavily-stocked stillwaters have proved to be a great way to introduce beginners to flyfishing. They provide the ideal place to learn the basics of casting, line management and fly presentation. Also, the capture of a few fish encourages the novice angler to continue in the sport. Youngsters, in particular, need success to maintain their interest. However, I try to avoid fisheries that have just been stocked, preferring something a little more challenging.

I catch many of my wild fish, or long-term resident stocked fish, from within a metre of the margins. At close range, I can often see the fish even when they are not rising. If no fish are visible I search the bankside pockets, under overhanging branches, in the pockets in front of rocks, along weed-beds and current seams, in fact any likely holding spot or patrol route. Of course, attractive holding sites are not confined to the margins, but they tend to be more concentrated along the water's edge. The close contact style of flyfishing, which I now generally use, requires very different techniques and tackle than for the far-off approach I used to use. As previously alluded to, stealth is of prime importance. I am a hunter stalking his prey. I am attired in a mix of drab greens, olives and browns. I try to make the most of any cover. This may involve using suitable backgrounds to avoid producing a fish-scaring silhouette, kneeling to cast (kneepads are frequently used) or cautiously wading into the river to lower my profile below the trout's window of view; internal reflection on the water surface limits the lowest angle at which a fish can see the above surface world (however this assumes a perfectly flat water-surface so should not be relied upon as a means of avoiding being seen by the fish). In addition, I move very slowly and avoid false casting as much as possible since fish are very sensitive to visible movements and unnatural vibrations in the water; not for me the metronome casting I so often see – where the angler repeatedly false casts prior to the final cast.

What of my choice of tackle? I no longer use stiff, super-fast-action rods with heavy lines. At close range, usually well under half a fly-line distance, I want delicacy and line control. My favoured rods are fairly soft, middle to tip action, facilitating short accurate casts including roll casts. On my local North Yorkshire Moors streams I usually opt for a one-weight of around 7 to 8 ft long, or in very confined, wooded brooks a 6 ft two-weight. On slightly larger, more open rivers like my local Driffield West Beck I'll use a 10 ft two-weight or 11 ft three-weight, whilst on bigger rivers like the Middle Wharfe, Scottish Tay or Slovenia's Soča I'll choose a 10 ft four-weight or 11 ft three-weight. On small to medium stillwaters I prefer either an 11 ft three-weight or 10 ft four-weight rod for the imitative style that I prefer to fishing with lures. Light lines and long rods give me the ability to maintain fine control over my line. With the longer rods I can more easily mend, reach-cast and keep the line off fast flows or awkward surface drift. The light lines also enhance line control and when necessary allow me to lift with minimal disturbance. If fishing at long distance (over 40 ft) I prefer double-taper or long-head weight-forward lines as I find the ability to lift off and cast without having to take in any running line, or false cast and virtually instantly redirect the next cast, can be critical on stillwaters when rainbows are cruising just below the surface mopping up buzzer pupae in the surface film. Furthermore, when one end of the line is worn I can reverse a double-taper line, doubling its life. I may have been born a Lancastrian, but having lived in Yorkshire for over two-thirds of my life I've acquired the thriftiness of a true Yorkshireman. A big advantage of close-range fishing is the improved ability to drop a fly accurately into the path of a feeding fish. Add to this the fact that light lines cause less disturbance when they land and you've got a winning combination. Couple the light line with a long leader (I generally use one of 12 to 18 ft/4 to 6 m) with the stealthy approach mentioned earlier and the fish will never know you are there till they are hooked. In recent years I have used long, light Tenkara rods, with a fixed line for much of my close-range fishing and I have also taken to the Italian Style of casting which allows me to fish with a line one to two weights lighter than the rod's designation plus a long leader. I will say more about Tenkara and Italian Style casting later.

What other advantages does this close-range approach have? Well, as mentioned earlier, you can see the fish far more easily. As a result, their precise

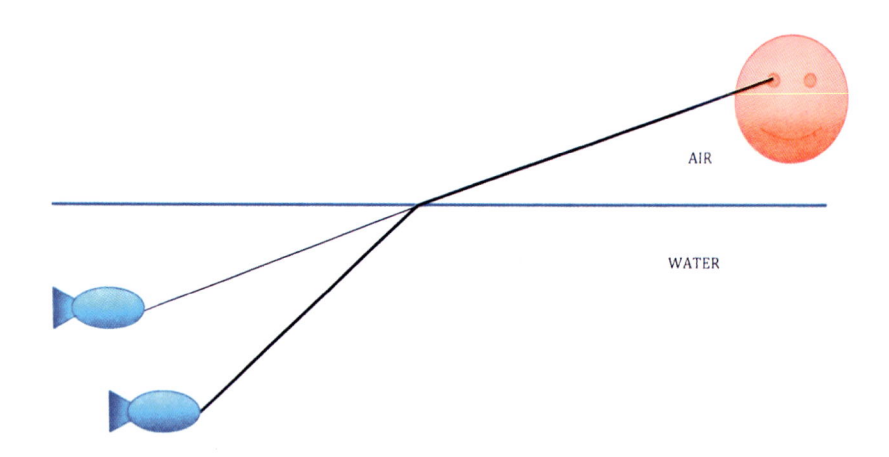

Light rays are refracted, making a fish appear to be nearer the surface and further away

position can be pinpointed (remember that due to refraction, the bending of light rays at the water surface, a visible fish will be closer and deeper in the water than it appears).

Furthermore, from their more easily observed behaviour it may be possible to surmise what they are feeding on. In addition, it may be possible to observe subsurface takes. I get a real kick out of watching a good brownie or grayling, just a few yards away, open its mouth and inhale my nymph or shrimp. Only a few days before writing this, on a small stillwater, near Driffield, several guys were casting their lures well out from the banks with little success. Meanwhile, I was stalking along the quieter banks looking for fish that were cruising along the marginal shelf, just a metre out. A small bloodworm or size 20 Pheasant Tail Nymph dropped accurately in their path was what the fish wanted on a day when others caught little. I had several fish including one of nearly 13 lb. The latter fish would never have been visible further out due to the fact that heavy overnight rain had coloured the water.

So, don't be reticent about casting right into the bank edge, particularly if

12 lb 14 oz rainbow cruising along the bank caught on a slow-sinking bloodworm

there is a profusion of overhanging bankside vegetation. Good fish will lie in inches of water if they feel secure. I once had a beautiful 2¾ lb wild brownie out of a local beck – from water less than a foot deep – by dropping a Pheasant Tail Nymph an inch from a floating mat of marginal canary reed grass.

FISH LIES

In rivers brown trout have favoured feeding lies. If such lies are in the immediate proximity of cover and are on the edge of a reliable food conveyor current the fish may spend much of their time there. However, some feeding sites may be many metres away from suitable resting places, in which case the fish may only take up residence there when there is a glut of food (eg a hatch of olives or a fall of black gnats). The location of these temporary types of feeding lie depends very much upon the food source. For example, *Caenis* nymphs are silt dwellers and on my North Yorkshire Moors streams hatches

Barry Parsons playing a grayling caught on a size 26 CdC aphid during leaf fall

and spinner falls mainly occur on the slower straights and in the deeper pools. A few seasons back I'd fished up a series of riffles on the Yorkshire Derwent with very limited success, when I noticed what looked like heavy thunder rain falling onto the slow, silted straight further upstream. Arriving there I found that the falling raindrops were actually the rises of hundreds of fish gathered to feed on a localised fall of *Caenis* spinners. Falls of aphids may also be localised, particularly in areas with high concentrations of overhanging sycamore trees. I know several such sites where, on a windy day in May or during the autumn leaf fall, I can expect fish to be rising to aphids. Knowing the location and timing of these food gluts is a vital ingredient for optimising flyfishing success.

On any given day a good starting point is, therefore, to have an idea of what the potentially vulnerable food source might be and where to expect concentrations of that food source. For example, in mid-April on the upper Yorkshire Derwent the main potential food sources will be large dark olives

Large dark olive

Typical area where large dark olives emerge early season

[LDO], small to medium sized stoneflies, black gnats and possibly the first hawthorn flies. The LDO hatches can be very unreliable, but the fish often move into good feeding lies well before the hatch starts. I have had several club members say how useless it is fishing this stream before the first stockies of the season are introduced in May. They complain of a lack of fish in a river that is actually stuffed with wildies. The reason for their early season failure is because they fish in the wrong places. They concentrate their efforts in the body of the slow, deep pools, just those places where the stockies congregate, since they are most like the stock ponds they've been reared in. The LDOs tend to emerge from the fast riffles, particularly those with a good growth of weed (*Ranunculus* or *Fontinalis*) (water buttercup or water moss). By 11am the wild trout gather at the pool heads, where the shallows drop off into slightly deeper water. This area provides shelter from the main flow, whilst the current brings a constant supply of emerging LDO duns from noon till mid-afternoon.

What about the black gnats and hawthorn flies? These are most vulnerable on warm, sunny, breezy days. In good years vast clouds may be seen sheltering behind windbreaks (trees and hedges). Being relatively poor fliers, many crash-land in the river where they subside into the surface film, they are easy prey for the fish. Find such a spot then search for foam lines, seams and eddies on the edge of the main flow, in fact find anywhere where this food source is being funnelled or trapped and you are in for a bonanza session.

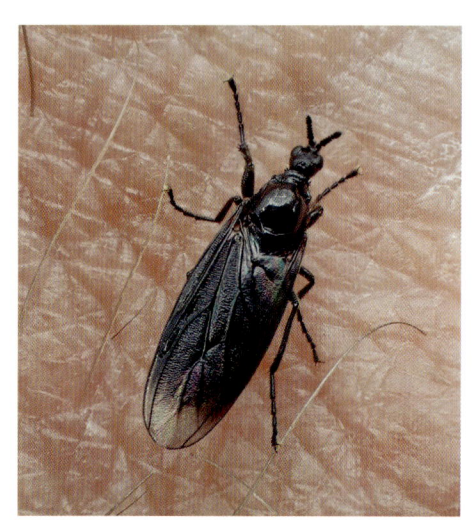

Black gnat, female   *Hawthorn fly, male*

SOME THOUGHTS ON WATERCRAFT AND THE LOCATION OF FISH

Pool heads and tails are always good places to find fish throughout the season. The former are well-oxygenated: the broken water providing good cover for the fish, usually with deep water bolt-holes close at hand and there is a constant inflow, potentially bringing food with it. The latter may seem less favourable locations, but the water from the pool all funnels through the shallower tail concentrating any food items drifting out of the pool. Also, the good flow over clean gravel at pool tails provides an ideal habitat for many aquatic nymphs and larvae. Furthermore, the shallow water gives some protection from predation by otters and cormorants. Unfortunately, pool tails present two major problems. First is the difficulty of approaching the fish in such shallow water without spooking them and secondly it is a real challenge to avoid drag, since the angler fishing upstream is virtually always casting over faster water into slower water (the flow accelerates as it approaches the pool tail due to the decreasing depth). At dusk, and during darkness, shallow pool tails can become sites of intense feeding activity, with fish chasing fry, or skittering sedges, in water so shallow that during the day no self-respecting fish of any real size would be seen dead there. Darkness provides cover and a sense of security in the gin-clear, low water of summer spate rivers, so dusk, night and dawn may provide the best opportunity of good sport. Unfortunately, many clubs ban night fishing.

Large rocks create two pockets of calm water, one in front of and one behind the rock. These provide perfect spots for trout to ambush their prey. The one in front is often the deeper and provides the fish with a clear view of any food drifting towards it. If the main food bearing flow passes around these rocks so much the better. One of my best Cumbrian River Eamont trout, a three pounds plus wild fish, came from just in front of a submerged boulder, as did my best cutthroat trout (18½ in) on a trip to Yellowstone's Lamar River in 2009. Boulder-strewn rivers, like the upper Tees (above High Force) or Austria's Zembach, contain staggering stocks of wild trout because not only do they have good spawning gravels, but they have vast numbers of

Top: 5 lb 1 oz Driffield Beck trout   Above: 2 lb 10 oz Driffield Beck grayling

lies. On such rivers each trout has quite a small territory so they rarely reach a large size (a twelve-incher is a good fish), but the biomass of fish present is staggering. Don't always expect to see the subsurface rocks, particularly in peat-stained moorland streams or high water. A swirl or boil in the surface flow will betray their presence. Similarly weed-beds provide two potential feeding lies and their presence may be indicated (if not directly visible) by disturbances in the surface flow. In the summer of 2009, I had a 2 lb 10 oz grayling and a 5 lb 1 oz brown trout in consecutive casts from just such a spot behind a bed of *Ranunculus* on East Yorkshire's Driffield Beck.

Sheltered, bankside pockets next to the main flow are prime feeding spots and frequently hold the bigger fish. However, they often challenge the angler's ability to offer a drag-free presentation. A couple of seasons back, I had a cracking 2 lb 12 oz wild Cumbrian Eden brownie from just such a spot. It took a few casts to get a long enough drag-free drift, but it was worth the effort.

Where the flow passes beneath overhanging trees is another place to expect fish, even if the water seems too shallow. Trout love cover and on windy days a host of terrestrials (beetles, wood ants, caterpillars, etc) will be dislodged from the branches. Sadly, too many club work parties destroy all overhanging branches to facilitate easy casting. They don't seem to understand that there is no use being able to cast to a spot if the fish have vacated it for more sheltered sites (possibly on someone else's less well-maintained fishery).

Debris dams and submerged fallen trees are also too frequently cleared away by tidy-minded river-keepers and club work parties, yet they too are ideal shelters and food factories. Anyone doubting this should read the Wild Trout Trust's pamphlet on woody debris. When search-fishing I always risk a few casts in these snag-rich sites. The sacrifice of a few flies is worth the potential reward. On a September 2009 trip to Montana's Bitterroot River most of my cutthroat trout came from the edge of structure (submerged trees and debris dams). A couple of seasons back, whilst fishing a pool on the Yorkshire Rye, a colossal brownie (well over 7 lb) shot out from a submerged

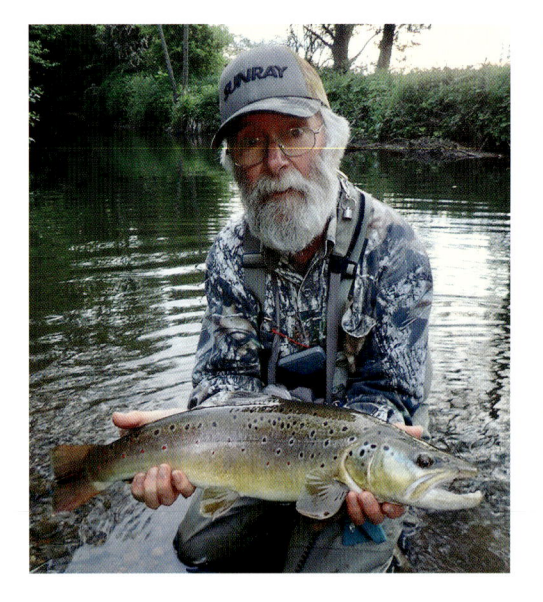

4 lb 12 oz wild trout, Yorkshire River Rye, caught from a small bankside pocket

tree and attacked the pound and a half trout I was playing, whilst my best trout from the Yorkshire Rye, a wild fish of 4 lb 12 oz, fell to a Daddy cast into a small pocket behind a clump of alder roots. Furthermore, on the upper Yorkshire Derwent there was a pool with a fallen tree in its midst that never failed to produce half-a-dozen good fish from amongst the submerged branches. Once the tree had gone I rarely caught a fish there.

Undercut banks are virtually always on the outside of bends next to a good flow (food conveyor belt) and they provide the ultimate in fish cover. On my local Oxfolds Beck, near Pickering, I've watched trout of well over 5 lb slowly melt away under some surprisingly deep overhangs. My best fish from this spot weighed exactly 4 lb. Sadly, the fishing on this lovely little limestone stream underwent a catastrophic decline due to pollution, siltation and predation by cormorants and I have not fished it since. In the summer of 2008, whilst fishing Austria's Krimmler Ache, I found that high water levels due to snow melt had pushed most of the fish into the margins. Fishing the undercuts proved very productive for both brown and brook trout.

Depressions in the riverbed, however small, can provide that little bit of shelter from the force of the main flow needed for a trout or grayling to take up station. I've often caught fish (some surprisingly big) from pockets 25 cm (10 in) deep in riffles no more than half that depth. I never ignore the "skinny water". I remember wading a 100 m long glide on Slovenia's River Soča, most

River Soča grayling

Glide, River Soča, Slovenia

Stuart Crofts fishing a Chernobyl Ant in middle of the far-bank foam

of which was only ankle deep; however, I found one tiny depression, no more than 3 m long and 2 m wide that held half-a-dozen big grayling.

Areas where two or more flows meet are focus points for food. Concentrations of food attract concentrations of fish. Grayling seem to love such spots, lying in the slower water beneath the main flow and eagerly rising for tempting morsels drifting in the faster surface flow.

On windy days surface insects may be blown against the windward bank, particularly olive duns with their large, sail-like wings. These concentrations of food are rarely ignored by the trout, which will line up against the bank, queuing for the feast.

Foam lanes are a sure sign that the currents are concentrating anything that is floating (bubbles and insects). Furthermore, eddies filled with foam show that food from the main flow is accumulating there. Expect spent spinners, half-drowned aphids, beetles, black gnats. The variety of species trapped there will depend on the time of day, time of year and nature of the river. Some flyfishers avoid casting into the foam, since it is hard to distinguish one's fly from the bubbles. Some think that the fish will never see their fly in all that mass of bubbles. Dry-flies with bright pink sight posts solve the first problem. The second isn't a problem: the fish can easily distinguish your fly from the bubbles and any other debris thanks to millions of years of evolution which have adapted them perfectly to their habitat and to find food items.

Trout caught by Stuart in the foam patch

So, next time you are down at the river, look and think. Where would you choose to be if you were a feeding trout or grayling? You'd want an easily accessible food supply, cover from predators close by, plenty of oxygen and a place where you didn't have to work too hard swimming against the current. Find all these things together and there's sure to be a fish there. Of course, the easiest way to find feeding lies is to look for rising fish. That is why dry-fly fishing is much more straightforward than nymph fishing, because you know where the fish is and that it is in a feeding mood. All you've got to do then is ascertain what it is feeding on and present your imitation correctly. Straightforward, but not necessarily easy!

STEALTH

The flyfisher's second objective, once the fish have been located, is to get close enough to cast to them without scaring them.

Fish have very small brains and are therefore incapable of rational thought and anglers who see themselves as "hunters of the wily trout" are deluding themselves. Despite being "thick" fish do have innate, reflex responses to aid survival and are capable of learning and the acquisition of conditioned reflexes that help them to avoid unpleasant, potentially harmful stimuli, whilst responding positively to pleasant, rewarding stimuli. As a result, they are not always easy to catch and the flyfisher must use his, or her, far superior brainpower to achieve consistent success. However, we must think at their level: think like a fish! There are just four things which are significant in the life of a fish; fear, food, sex and sleep. It sounds a bit like me, but in my case substitute flyfishing for sex (I'm getting a bit old for that)! Because they have such tiny brains, fish only seem to be able to cope with one of these occupations at a time. As a result, it is impossible to catch a fish preoccupied with mating or sleeping, or which has been scared.

Since we should not be fishing for fish that are involved in the act of courtship and mating, I'm not going to expand much on the topic of fish sex. Breeding fish need to be left alone to propagate more fish for us to catch. Anyway, fish sex is not terribly exciting, unless you're a fishery biologist, a fish farmer or an ethologist. Similarly, sleeping fish are not at all interesting to most of us. Like breeding fish, they don't scare easily and are impossible to catch. I regularly see them on my local chalk stream, virtually static, just above the bottom. I've learned to bypass them and look for those that are actively feeding.

I'm going to concentrate on a few things anglers do that scare fish or, more importantly, what we should do to avoid scaring them. Some fish are virtually impossible to scare. I've watched newly stocked rainbows milling around the bankside where anglers were fishing. They'd been attracted to

Soda Butte Creek, Yellowstone National Park, USA

the anglers by the expectation of a handful of pellets. These fish had been conditioned all their previous life to associate people with food. Furthermore, splashy, repeated casting actually attracts them, as does one of their companions thrashing about on the end of a line: to an inexperienced stock fish splashes are food pellets being thrown in and a thrashing companion is chasing after and competing for those pellets. On very heavily fished waters even the wild fish may become habituated to the presence of anglers. In September 2009, I fished a popular stretch of Soda Butte Creek in the north-east of Yellowstone National Park. The wild cutthroat trout would just separate to allow a wading angler a clear passage and then virtually immediately they'd go back to their original lies and continue feeding. With so many anglers around if they had persisted in reacting as normal wild trout do they would have died from malnutrition. They had learned that anglers wading and on the bank were not in themselves harmful. However, their reaction to flies was very different. They did not flee in response to a clumsy

Soda Butte Creek cutthroat trout

cast or a dragging fly, but even the slightest micro-drag resulted in the fly's rejection. Having learned that micro-dragging flies result in an unpleasant experience, rising fish even turned away when natural midges and upwing duns were buffeted by a gust of wind. I've seen the same on very heavily fished, catch-and-release, small stillwaters, where the stockie rainbows have become very challenging only falling for perfectly presented flies that adequately imitated natural foods.

Wild trout on lightly fished waters are a completely different kettle of fish. They can be extremely spooky and once scared can take quite a time to settle down and come back on feed. So, what scares such fish?

- Sight of the angler, particularly movement.
- Any shadow or unexpected object that passes across the water.
- Any unusual vibration in the water.
- Any other fish close by that shows panic (unless it is a small food species).

The author keeping low, Thornton Beck, North Yorkshire

Let's deal with each of these:

1. Stealth can be of paramount importance. Be aware that scared fish don't always bolt when they've seen the angler. Sometimes they will just drift slowly out of sight into cover or they'll merely stop feeding and stay on station. What can we do to stop being seen?
2. Approach from downstream of the fish, casting up or up and across. This will hopefully keep us in the narrow zone that is outside the vision of our quarry (although there is evidence from photographic studies by Don Stazicker and Peter Hayes suggesting that such a zone may not exist).
3. Keep low by crouching, kneeling or deep wading. If bank fishing, use a screen of bankside cover whenever possible. I know it can make casting difficult, but it is better that than casting to where the fish was before you spooked it. I often use neoprene kneepads to protect my waders and knees when kneeling.

Kneeling behind cover, Driffield Beck, East Yorkshire

4. Wear drab, camouflaged clothing so you blend with the background.
5. When fishing in the open try to keep a suitable background such as bushes or a high bank behind you, so you are not silhouetted against the sky.
6. Fish broken water where the fish's window to the outside world is disrupted. You'll be surprised how close you can get to fish in a tumbling riffle.
7. Whether on land or wading move like a snail, or more realistically like a stalking lion, cheetah or leopard. It has been shown that the first trigger by which trout fry recognise food is its movement. Trout eyesight is particularly sensitive to movement. A large portion of their brain is dedicated to vision.
8. The last, least-practical, option is to fish at long range, which introduces a lot of problems. Accurate casting, avoiding drag, seeing takes and hooking the fish all become much more difficult. I like to be no more than 30 ft (10 m) from my target, much closer if possible. On a trip to fish the small streams of the Smoky Mountains on the Tennessee/North Carolina

The author using cover, and perfect camouflage, whilst Tenkara fishing in Austria

border in 2010, many of my brook and rainbow trout were taken at a range of about 9 to 15 ft (3 to 5 m).

If you have to fish with the sun behind you, keeping low and using cover will reduce the risk of casting your shadow over the water. One real no-no is false casting over the fish. All too often I see other flyfishers imitating metronomes. If you have to false cast, for example when working out enough line to reach a distant fish, do it in a different direction to that of your target; then redirect your final cast. On rivers, when fishing upstream, shorten your drift so you take in no more line than you can shoot without having to false cast. On wide rivers, when I'm not too close to my target and where smooth flows ensure that drag is not too much of a potential problem, I often choose to cast across the flow (usually slightly down and across with a slack-line cast so I can track the rod and achieve a reasonably long drag-free drift). It is then easy to lift off and recast with no false casts. (This is only true if fishing within the range of the belly of a weight-forward line, or with a double-taper line.) Long leaders help to reduce the risk of the fly-line scaring the fish. This is particularly important when fishing directly upstream or directly downstream. My standard leader length is from 12 ft to 18 ft depending on the size of river and how close a range I expect to fish.

The lateral lines of fish contain baro-receptors that are incredibly sensitive to vibrations/pressure changes in the water. Whilst the twitch of a drowning daddy-long-legs (cranefly) is enough to alert a trout to the presence of food, clumsy wading or the heavy fall of a fly-line can cause panic in wild trout. Unusual movements/vibrations could be predators. Stocked fish may well be unaware of this but wild fish will often panic instantly. The reason why many anglers making the transition from put-and-take stillwaters to rivers frequently find catching fish difficult is that they scare the wild river fish before they ever get a chance to cast to them. I've known days when the fish on my local chalk stream have fled at the delicate landing of a one-weight line and 18 ft leader. This has usually occurred when their threshold of fear has been lowered by recent predation by cormorants or disturbance by other anglers. Only cast aggressively if the fish are expecting large food items to crash onto the water; for example, as I did in autumn 2009, when large grasshoppers were active on a hot afternoon on Montana's Bitterroot River. Even then, you only want the fly to crash-land, not the fly-line, so it is important to stop the rod hard and early, holding the rod tip high so that the fly kicks over fast, but the fly-line is held back, to land more delicately (or even better not land at all), alternatively use the Italian Style of casting which aims to land the fly first. "High-sticking" or Tenkara fishing (at very close range) is a great way of ensuring that the fly-line never lands on the water and is also a very good way of reducing drag to a minimum. If possible, fish from the bank to avoid the inevitable disturbance caused by wading. If you have to wade, approach your prey with the stealth of a heron. On one of my local small streams some club members, who mainly fish the lower, stocked beats, complain how hard the upper, un-stocked, beats are. My catch rate on the upper beats over the last twenty seasons has been three times that on the lower ones. The reason? I used the utmost caution in my approach to the fish. I used the lightest line possible and as long a leader as was practical, presented with the utmost delicacy. An alternative to long leaders is Stuart Crofts' approach, involving the use of a short (4 ft) furled leader to which is attached about 2 ft of 4x tippet and 2 to 3 ft of 6x tippet. This set-up facilitates very accurate casting and lands extremely delicately, but is a little less forgiving when casting into a wind than the aggressively tapered copolymer leaders I usually use. A plus point for the use of furled leaders is their incredible suppleness, which significantly reduces drag.

Finally, when you see a target fish always check that there is not a nearer one that you might spook and that could spread its fear should you scare it. If you are working your way upstream always go for the tail-end-Charlies first. When you hook them, bully them downstream so they don't disturb the fish above them. If there is a particularly big fish at the head of a pool and you just have to get him first then it might be better to approach from upstream (if club rules allow downstream fishing and if other factors make it feasible). On arrival at a swim avoid entering the river, or lake, until you've checked the margins in front of you. Brown trout love the margins where they can find cover under tree roots, overhanging vegetation or undercut banks. All too often a careless approach will scare off the best fish of the day.

Two PB fish
8 lb 5 oz trout and 10 lb 9 oz barbel where fly choice and presentation were important

2

SOME THOUGHTS ON TACTICS

PRESENTATION

What is more important, the fly or presentation? There are no hard and fast rules, only generalisations... There are too many variables for flyfishing to be an exact science. However, I believe presentation is usually more important than fly choice. Too much time can be spent seeking a "magic" fly-pattern. A friend, new to flyfishing, goes through fads: first he only fished the egg fly; then bloodworms; recently it's poppers. On the right day he catches fish, but often his magic fly fails. Sure, some flies are better than others and sometimes the choice of fly can be critical. It's illogical fishing a streamer or lure when the rainbows are rising like mad to tiny emerging buzzers/midges, yet I see this regularly on my local stillwaters.

When fish are keyed-on to a specific food source it can be vital to use a fly with the correct trigger(s), usually, size, basic shape and, sometimes, colour. However, trout are opportunistic and generally take anything resembling food. I recently caught a trout containing mayfly nymphs and duns, beetles, black gnats and a crayfish – a real mixed bag! Preoccupation only occurs when a specific food item is abundant, particularly if it is small; e.g. *Caenis*, aphids and micro-buzzers. Even then there is not one magic fly, several similar patterns being equally effective.

On stillwaters when fish are mopping up micro-buzzer pupae, I'll

Size 28 Wire Buzzer Pupa   *Size 24 IOBO Humpy*

Size 30 Minimalistic Micro Midges

confidently fish any one of my own micro-buzzer pupae patterns, a Wire Buzzer Pupa, a Stripped Quill Bead-head Buzzer or a Sawyer Pheasant Tail Nymph, as long as it's size 24 or smaller. If they are taking adult midges, I'll use a size 24 to 30 IOBO Humpy, Shuttlecock, Wyatt's Deer Hair Emerger or Hackle-less Black Gnat, or my own Minimalistic Micro Midge (MMM), with equal confidence.

However, what is vital with small imitative patterns is a totally drag-free drift. Many times, I've watched fish approach my fly only to reject it

River Soča, Slovenia and a Soča grayling

at the last moment because of virtually indiscernible micro-drag. Even stockies on heavily fished, catch-and-release waters soon wise up, becoming highly discriminating.

In river dry-fly fishing the ability to achieve a drag-free drift is usually of paramount importance. In September 2005, I fished for grayling on the Soča, and other Slovenian rivers. During the early morning flurry of stonefly activity it did not matter whether I fished a size 14 F fly, CdC Spider, Wonder-wing Stonefly or IOBO Humpy. What did matter was presentation. I regularly watched grayling follow my dry-fly for up to 15 ft before deciding to take, or reject my offering. To delay drag required combination tactics. Fishing down and across proved to be the best angle of approach: a leader of 15 to 18 ft was used in conjunction with a 9 ft rod (10 ft would have been better); a combined dump-and-reach-cast was followed by tracking the rod downstream and sometimes even a step or two downstream to extend the drag-free drift. Even so, it was often necessary to cover a fish several times to achieve an acceptable drift and fool it. Even on my local Yorkshire small streams, at short range and with less complex currents, I usually prefer a long rod to hold the line above awkward flows and leaders of 12 ft plus (see my thoughts on Tenkara, p 97).

Other factors affecting drag are the suppleness of the leader and tippet, the size of the fly and whether it has a submerged body. Trials with furled leaders show they are incredibly supple and appear to delay drag a little longer than stiffer copolymer, however they have an infuriating habit of wrapping around the rod tip which can be a problem, particularly with long rods. I use the finest, most flexible tippet I can practically use, normally 6x (3.5 lb). With really small flies, 22 to 30, I sometimes drop to 7 or 8x (2 to 2½lb). Controversially, I don't bother to apply sinkant to my tippet since fine tippet is virtually impossible to sink and I find it makes no difference to the fish. Many thousands of trout and grayling have fallen to my dry-flies over recent years despite a floating tippet.

Large flies drag less, having more mass and more surface area in contact with the surface film. Klinkhåmers and semi-submerged patterns drag even less since the water resistance they generate helps to anchor them.

One day in autumn 2005, on Oxfolds Beck near Pickering, grayling were rising to olives, but a multiplicity of swirling currents flowing over the weed fronds caused unavoidable drag. My dry-fly was ignored! How was I to present an acceptable offering? My solution was to attach a nymph to a New Zealand Dropper from my dry-fly in the hope that the grayling might also be feeding on ascending nymphs. It worked! Slight drag made the nymph look alive!

There are always exceptions to the rule. Mayfly duns, sedges and daddy-long-legs can be quite active and a dragged or twitched fly will often score more heavily than a static one. Over a number of years, I had limited success during *Caenis* hatches despite a river alive with feeding fish. In 2006 my friend Steve Donohue found that, during an intense *Caenis* hatch, a dragged Griffiths Gnat would induce take after take. He "bagged-up", catching 40 trout in an hour. This tactic has worked for me, too, in recent years.

Their highly sensitive lateral lines of baro-receptors, which detect vibrations, alert fish not only to danger, but also live food. In Florida, whilst fishing with floating rubber-legged spiders and poppers for bluegills and large-mouth bass, a fly cast to the edge of the reeds, or into a pocket in the weeds, is left static for a moment before being twitched. This is usually followed by a sharp sucking sound and disappearance of the fly, the strike resulting in the typical jagging of a bluegill, or a large-mouth bass exploding out of the water, followed by a battle which is often more aerial than aquatic. Sometimes the static

Bluegill (top) and Large-mouth bass (above) caught on foam poppers, Florida

The author releasing a rainbow trout, River Soča, Slovenia

fly is taken, but more often the twitch triggers the take (see also my comments on Tenkara, p 97).

On stillwaters there are times when an Olive Damsel stripped back in long, quite fast, pulls has out-fished anything else. At other times, just a tiny movement may be all that is required. Recently I was fishing two Bloodworms close to the bottom. My point fly was regularly catching on weed and after a brief pause was being pulled free by the surface drift. Most of my takes occurred just as the point fly pulled free causing the static dropper fly to come to life.

When I visited Slovenia's River Soča, one of the most effective tactics for the rainbows was to cast a heavy nymph well upstream with a combined slack-line/dump cast and upstream reach, sometimes followed by a further mend to allow the fly to sink well down. Then, as the fly reached the fish's position downstream, I allowed the current to swing and lift the fly. This tactic/presentation accounted for numerous rainbows up to 22 in in length.

Let's consider an aspect of presentation linked to fly design. That is how and where, in or on the surface, the fly rests. Rising fish may be taking insects which are standing high and dry on the water's surface film: then a conventional collar-hackled dry-fly may be required (if you can get it to sit high up, which requires a very delicate landing). In my experience this tends to be the exception rather than the rule. Most surface feeders will be found to be taking insects emerging through or trapped in the surface film. Then what is needed is an emerger pattern that sits in the surface, possibly with its body submerged (Klinkhåmer, Wyatt's Deer Hair Emerger, or Shuttlecock), or a drowned insect pattern semi-submerged in the surface (Spent Spinner, Parachute pattern, Hawthorn Fly or Foam Beetle). What about subsurface flies? There are times when the trout and grayling want a nymph, bug, or spider that is dead-drifting. However, often I've had to give them suitable, often subtle, movement to simulate life to induce takes. Frank Sawyer and Oliver Kite were masters at this style of fishing. When Czech-nymphing many takes come at the end of the drift when the current is lifting the flies, or when the angler purposefully lifts prior to recasting. The same is true when trotting bait for grayling; takes often come as the float is held back, lifting the bait enticingly. Traditional Tenkara anglers use a number of techniques involving subtle movements of their Reversed Hackle Spider (Sakasa Kebari) flies.

Depth is an important aspect of presentation. In winter there are times when grayling are

Black Ant Sakasa Kebari

reticent about lifting even a foot off the bottom to take a fly. There are ways to achieve the required depth. Weighted flies with tungsten beads, lead underbodies, wire bodies and slim, smooth profiles sink fast. The grayling usually don't mind whether I fish a leaded shrimp, weighted nymph or Peeping Caddis so long as it bumps the bottom. Another option is to pinch a split shot onto the point and fish a small or unweighted fly on a dropper, paternoster style. This has two advantages; firstly, the inevitable snag up means only the loss of a shot and secondly an un-weighted fly has "life", wavering in the current unhindered by gravity. Split-shot can be added above the fly, but I prefer the former set-up. Long, fine, parallel tippets/leaders aid sinking and here fluorocarbon may help. (I don't like fluorocarbon because it does not degrade in UV light and so any fluorocarbon that is left hanging from trees etc after a miscast is a permanent hazard to wildlife.) I've tried sinking leaders, but find them awkward to cast with in the heavier weights and bite detection can be a problem. For Czech-nymphing braid is a potential leader material, being very thin for its breaking strain and, being non-stretchy, unseen bites may be felt.

What if the fish are higher in the water? When rainbows are feeding on emerging buzzers I need a fly within the top foot of the water. Then I fish a small buzzer, or Pheasant Tail Nymph on a New Zealand Dropper under a dry-fly, or suspended from a greased semi-curly, tri-colour monofilament indicator, or suspended from a greased leader. I've unsuccessfully tried Parasol Buzzers which to others seemed to be a potentially magic fly. The use of the controversial "bung" method on stillwaters is so successful because it allows a nymph, bloodworm or buzzer to be suspended and fished very slowly at the cruising/feeding depth of the fish, thus ensuring the fly is constantly in the feeding zone, but the indicators that are used tend to be quite large and taking fish sometimes feel the resistance and expel the fly; furthermore fish often take the bung. Another alternative is to suspend the fly or flies from a New Zealand wool or yarn indicator that has been treated with floatant: this causes

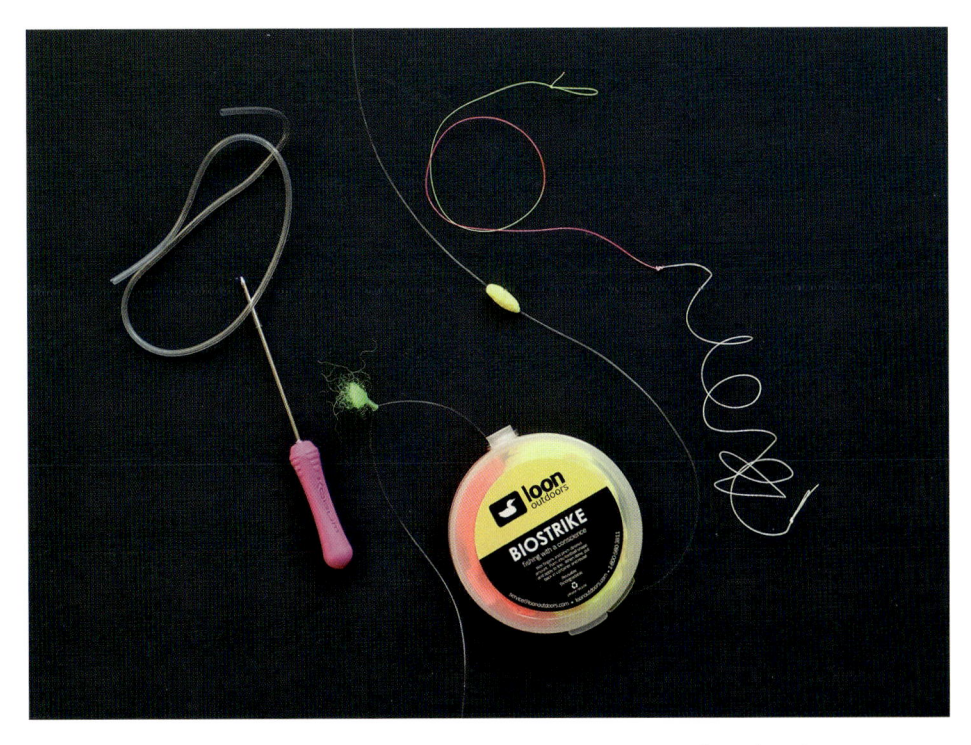

Indicators: New Zealand wool, Loon buoyant putty, greased semi-curly mono

less resistance to a taking fish and is easily slid up or down the leader to vary the depth at which your flies fish.

Another aspect of presentation is how the fly lands. Often it is important that the fly, leader and line land as softly as possible. In bright, low water conditions on Driffield Beck I've watched trout flee as even a one-weight line landed. As a result, I fish with as long a leader and as light a line as possible, often a delicate presentation, Micro Thin one-weight line or micro nymph line (see my thoughts on Italian Style casting, p 104). When fishing heavy nymphs I try to pitch them well upstream of the fish to avoid disturbance. Nevertheless, there are times when a fly landing heavily will be positively pounced on by a trout. Such conditions usually coincide with windy days when beetles or caterpillars are falling from overhanging trees, or when stockies have been recently introduced.

If you are one of those anglers in search of the magic fly I hope you find it, but, in the meantime, don't discount good presentation. The nearest I've found to a magic fly is Jack Tucker's IOBO Humpy (IOBO stands for It Oughta Be Outlawed). Even that only works effectively when carefully and thoughtfully presented and fished at the right times. All the best flyfishers and coarse fishers are sticklers when it comes to presentation!

Jack Tucker's CdC IOBO Humpy

DRAG

Drag can be literally and metaphorically a real drag. It can be the kiss of death to success, particularly for the dry-fly fisherman. Its cause is simple; the leader and fly-line cross currents with different flow rates, or the flow swings the line from a fixed point (the rod tip). As a result, a force on the terminal end of the tippet (a pull or push; usually a pull) causes the fly to move unnaturally.

This is mainly a problem on rivers and particularly those with complex surface flows created by the turbulence around and over rocks and weedbeds, or the uneven flow around bends. However, stillwater anglers also need to be aware of drag since stillwaters are rarely actually still! On my local stillwater, which has a slight flow, I have repeatedly watched rainbows inspect my Shuttlecock Buzzer and then swirl away in alarm as the wind or drag has caused a tiny amount of cross current drift. Slack-line casts, and a careful choice of fishing position with respect to the wind direction, can significantly reduce these problems. Many stillwater anglers advocate casting across the wind with buzzers and letting the bow in the line swing the flies around. However, I have noticed the same adverse response to subsurface buzzers dragging across the flow as to dry-flies dragging; nine times out of ten my local rainbows prefer them dead-drifted, or fished on the drop. Fishing into the wind on stillwaters can help avoid drag when fishing dries or buzzers just subsurface, since any flies fished on, in, or near to the surface will drift naturally with the surface flow. However, if this tactic is used with deeply fished nymphs and buzzers they will be dragged in the opposite direction to the undertow! On clear waters I often check the surface and subsurface flows/currents by throwing in two pieces of rolled up paper tissue; one dry to float and one soaked to sink. I then watch their relative progress. If there is too much disparity and the fish prove to be fussy (eg long-term residents) I'll move to another part of the lake where I can more easily achieve the correct presentation. I should add that freshly stocked fish may actually be attracted to a dragging fly since once their regular feed of pellets has stopped they have to test anything that might be food to try and satisfy their hunger.

Grayling, in particular, seem to be put off taking a dry-fly by even a trace of micro-drag. On my local Yorkshire rivers and on Slovenian rivers I have frequently watched grayling rise to a fly only to sink slowly back to the riverbed when they detected the slightest unnatural movement of the fly. I have had most frustration when fishing with size 22 to 30 midge imitations. At first, I put down my repeated missed takes to Bernard Benson's hypothesis (put into print by Oliver Edwards) that the grayling, because of their protruding upper lip, create a pressure wave on approaching the fly, which pushes it away. The Klinkhåmer's high hooking rate can be explained by the fact that the submerged abdomen anchors the fly in the surface film, stopping it from being pushed away as the grayling take it. However, I now question this hypothesis – logical though it is; I suspect that the anchoring of a submerged body in the surface resists/reduces drag resulting in fewer aborted rises. You might well say, "Who is this guy to question the observations of much better qualified anglers than he is?" What evidence do I have to support my alternative hypothesis? Well, my problems with missed takes have been much reduced when either:

1. I have been able to prevent micro-drag by slack-line casting, reach-casting or upstream-mending.
2. I have combined the above with a cast across, or across and downstream, using a long rod (10 ft or longer), then tracked the rod downstream to extend my drag-free drift.
3. I have been able to position myself so that my line and leader have not been crossing conflicting, drag-inducing currents.
4. I have fished at very short range such that, by holding the rod tip high, no fly-line and the minimum of leader/tippet has been on the water and therefore vulnerable to vagaries of the current.
5. The use of very long leaders, 15 ft plus with extra fine tippet, of 7 or 8x, has significantly reduced drag. I always use copolymer tippet rather than the much stiffer fluorocarbon to help delay drag. I have also used very supple furled leaders to good effect. The use of finer tippet can often increase an angler's chances of tempting finicky fish to take his or her fly. Many attribute the increased success of this method to the fact that fish cannot see the thinner tippet as readily. I don't think this is the reason: I believe that thinner, more supple tippet material is more effective because it significantly reduces drag.
6. The grayling have been prepared to take larger flies, such as Sedges and Klinkhåmers that are less affected by drag since they have more of a grip on the water surface.

I suspect that, as with many things, my hypothesis is not the complete answer; probably missed grayling takes are due to the interaction of a number of factors.

It needs to be remembered, however, that there are times when trout and even grayling are positively attracted to drag. These are times when drag makes the fly behave like the natural, or triggers an aggression reflex as so often happens with rainbows which will often attack anything that moves. Many surface and subsurface organisms just dead-drift in an inert, passive manner, but others struggle in the surface film, flutter across the surface whilst emerging or laying eggs, or swim actively across the current or up to the surface.

It is possible to induce savage takes from trout by twitching a Daddy-long-legs. This simulates the insect struggling to escape from entrapment by the surface tension. I am convinced that the movement alerts fish to the Daddy's presence, the vibrations being detected by the lateral line sensors. The trout then sees the fly behaving perfectly naturally and takes with confidence. One August evening I arrived at the Yorkshire Derwent to find the river dead. Not a rise was to be seen. During the summer the rules of the club state that members are expected to fish the dry-fly, so on went a Paraloop Pheasant Tail Spinner, my most effective evening pattern. An hour produced only a couple of small fish. I tied on a Daddy but it proved equally ineffective until I started giving it a twitch every so often. To say the sport was explosive is an understatement. I ended up catching over twenty fish, both wildies and stockies.

Mayflies and sedges may be twitched in a similar manner, or even dragged across the surface to great effect. Dragged sedges and moths, such as the late Dick Walker's Chicken (ghost swift moth) are particularly effective at dusk and into the night, where allowed. I can remember one evening on the River Tar in Eire when it was too dark to see a rise. The fish were still taking Blue-winged Olive (BWO) Spinners, but I could not have fished a spinner effectively in the dark. The dragged sedge was the answer and for half-an-hour I had a take virtually every cast. Many tugs were missed, but a good number of fish stayed on.

The classic use of drag to induce takes is when nymph fishing. Frank Sawyer and Oliver Kite were masters of the induced take. Oliver Kite even took fish on a bare hook with just a blob of wound copper wire, to simulate a nymph's thorax, whilst blindfolded. Many of my best grayling have come to weighted nymphs or shrimps cast above and beyond the fish, then lifted to simulate life. Recently, on the Driffield West Beck, I had a number of good grayling on a small, black Bead-headed Hare's Ear Nymph. The river was very low and clear and the sun bright. The shoal took no notice of the dead-drifted Nymph, despite repeated presentations, but as soon as I gave the fly life, by twitching it upwards and across the stream, the fish showed interest. Most times I had follows, but when I got the presentation just right I got confident takes. Those fish were very fussy and took a lot of working on before they were convinced that my fly was food.

The induced take with the nymph simulates the active nymphs of the *Baetis* group, but many other subsurface organisms are also active swimmers. Sedge pupae use powerful paddle-like legs to actively swim to the surface when emerging. The freshwater shrimp (*Gammarus*) can be fished in the same way. Other patterns to fish actively include fry imitations; crayfish, which either crawl, or propel themselves backwards in short, sharp jerks; *Corixas* and water beetles, which also swim in short jerky motion. Leeches swim with a smooth undulating motion that is well-imitated by marabou lures and Zonkers.

POCKET-WATER FISHING

They say variety is the spice of life and certainly there is nothing I like better than to fish new waters, particularly if they are different in character from my local ones and doubly so if the fish are truly wild. My home rivers, the chalk streams of East Yorkshire and the small spate streams of the North Yorkshire Moors, are great, but I've fished them so often that they have become very predictable. I know the lies and the tactics to use. I've even got to know some of the fish personally: there's Freda, the big Driffield Beck grayling with a distinctive spot behind her right gill cover – I've caught her four times, and Fred, a three pounds plus brownie that always takes up the same feeding spot when there is a strong westerly wind. A move out of one's comfort zone can work wonders when it comes to advancing one's fishing skills and enjoyment. Fishing tumbling, wild, boulder-strewn pocket water has done just that for me.

My first real experience of this type of fishing was during a 1900-mile bicycle tour of the Yukon and Alaska, in the summer of 2000. I took a multi-piece fly-rod and a small box of assorted flies. I fished a wide range of waters from the massive Kluane Lake, on the Alaska Highway near the Canadian/Alaskan border (where I caught some good grayling and small lake trout), to the tiny Ruffus Creek in the Wrangles/St Elias Wilderness Park of Alaska (a mere 6 ft wide, but full of Dolly Varden char). The river that stands out in my memory is Brushkana Creek, on the Denali Highway. I'd never seen such boulder-strewn tumbling water before and was unsure how to tackle such a maelstrom. I had no waders, but by dropping a bead-headed Nymph into marginal pockets, and into the calmer water behind nearby boulders, letting my Nymph sink then lifting to induce a take, I managed to extract a fair number of grayling up to about ten inches. Tiny fish, but great fun!

I had to wait until I visited Austria in 2007 for my next experience of real pocket-water. My fishing buddy, Steve, had told me of the wonderful fishing he'd experienced on a small stream, called the Zembach, near the ski resort of Mayrhofen, so, a trip was arranged for early July. My first view of the river was just as I had pictured it: gin-clear water tumbling and churning around a mass of boulders, with the occasional pool. The weather was baking hot and the sun bright; not very encouraging! Furthermore, there were no rising fish and very little fly-life, just a few daddies and hawthorn flies (Yes! Hawthorn flies in July!). However, it transpired that every boulder had a resident fish in front of it and another behind it and they were eager to launch an assault on any dry-fly that came their way, so long as it was well presented (drag-free). So eager were they that I even had one fish follow my Daddy down a metre-high waterfall before taking it. During our two days there Steve Donahue and I caught an obscene number of wild brown trout to just over 14 in, plus a few similar sized

(Above) Zembach, Austria   (Below) Krimmler Ache, Austria

Stuart Crofts Tenkara-fishing pocket-water on the upper River Tees

stream-bred rainbows. A move to Mittersill gave us the opportunity to fish a couple of other rivers with sections of pocket-water, the little Amerbach and the Krimmler Ache. The latter was full of stunning, naturalised brook trout, again up to 14in, plus brown trout and a few grayling.

After experiencing this type of fishing, I was keen for more, but a meagre pension limits my opportunities for travelling abroad. Where could I find such water within striking range of East Yorkshire? Fortunately, I remembered Geoffrey Bucknall's articles in *Fly Fishing & Fly Tying* magazine about the upper Tees. A dull, cold (8°C), breezy day in mid-May 2008 found Steve Donohue and I on the banks of the Tees above High Force. The river was like a very big Zembach, except for the lack of trees and the heavily peat-stained water. The other difference was that, from about 11am till mid-afternoon, we saw a good mixed hatch of medium olives, olive uprights, iron blues and large brook duns, plus a few stoneflies, to which the fish eagerly rose. We both lost count of the exact number of fish we caught: beautiful dark-coloured, big-spotted

Typical upper Tees trout

wild brown trout up to a little over 12 in and all to the dry-fly. Further visits have confirmed the upper Tees fish to be very free risers.

Pocket-water fishing with the dry-fly poses a number of challenges. The complex, swirling, currents make the avoidance of drag very difficult. My first approach to combatting this problem was to fish at very short range with a long rod, a 10 ft three-weight, an 18 ft leader and virtually no fly-line out of the rod tip. I was virtually dapping, high-sticking or Czech-nymphing with a dry-fly. However, I was still getting drag because too much of the leader was on the water and therefore subjected to the vagaries of the currents. I found that shortening my leader to between 12 and 14 ft worked better, since I could hold all but the last foot or so of tippet off the water. A potential problem with this close combat style of fishing is the spooking of one's quarry. Fortunately, the turbulent, broken water surface helps to mask the angler's approach but, even so, great stealth is necessary and, with this in mind, Steve and I have both invested in kneepads so we can keep a low profile where necessary. If you ever see an old, bearded guy crawling over the boulders in the Tees, it'll probably be me. Of course, there are times when a longer cast is necessary. Then it is vital to work out the best angle of approach and exactly where to land the fly-line and leader to delay the dreaded drag. Then is the time to put in mends and reaches (often in conjunction with rod tracking if the cast is made across or downstream). These are not the kind of waters to be constrained within the confines of the classic upstream dry-fly method. Whilst an approach from downstream and casting up certainly reduces the risk of scaring the fish, other factors may render this angle of approach impossible. Massive boulders or deep holes in the otherwise shallow stream bed may be in the way, whilst wind funnelling down open valleys may dictate the only possible line of approach. On a recent trip to the upper Tees, a nightmare wind was gusting downstream along one section of river, whilst further on it was blowing upstream. Presentation was incredibly difficult since when I held my rod up, to keep line off the water, the wind just whisked the fly skywards. My only choice was to try to direct my line so that as much as possible landed on water flowing at the same rate and with enough slack in the system to delay drag for as long as possible. Steve and I managed about 30 fish apiece, despite the conditions, but we both agreed that it was hard and at times frustrating trying to get the presentation right. Having mentioned the problem of wind when using this short line dry-fly method to both Stuart Wardle and Stuart Crofts (both of whom have fished for the England Rivers Flyfishing Team) they suggested another answer to the problem; the use of the duo or nymph on a New Zealand Dropper method, in which the nymph anchors the dry-fly, resisting drag due to the wind's action on the leader.

I much prefer to fish the dry-fly when I can and, fortunately, in these shallow, fast rivers the fish seem to be looking up much of the time. What kind of dry-flies are needed for this type of fishing? My first priority is that I should be able to see them on the turbulent, foam-flecked surface. Secondly, they must float well and, thirdly, they must be acceptable to the fish. If there is no obvious hatch a size 14 Black Gnat/Hawthorn or Black Klinkhåmer is probably as good a choice as any. Often fly choice is far less important than presentation. However, beware the pitfall of thinking that these relatively small, hungry fish, in apparently food-poor waters, will always take any offering. On my early May 2009 trip to the upper Tees there was a steady hatch of large dark olives and olive uprights. By noon I'd already had several fish to my size 14 Hi-viz Parachute Olive, so when I came across a small pod of risers I was confident of success. After suffering repeated rejections, I was thinking that the strong wind was preventing me from presenting the fly properly. Then I noticed that amongst the larger flies there were one or two tiny iron blue duns (virtually invisible on the dark, windswept surface). A change to a size 20 Hi-viz Iron Blue did the trick and I had three of the half-dozen risers before the iron blues stopped hatching and the fish stopped rising, despite the onset of a blizzard hatch of large brook duns which were completely ignored. Further up the river I found fish that were taking the large brook duns. Why the earlier fish weren't interested in them I don't know. That's the fascination of this game; there's so much to learn; so much we don't know or understand! Another good pattern when there is no hatch is the Hi-viz Furled-body Paradaddy, a buoyant, easily seen Daddy pattern. Contrary to some people's misconceptions daddies (craneflies) are active throughout the trout season and although trout don't see them often (other than during the usual late summer glut) they certainly know what they are and when not preoccupied with other food sources (in my experience preoccupation is rare) they will rarely refuse a Daddy.

Hi-vis Paradaddy

I've also had fabulous pocket-water fishing in the Smoky Mountains National Park in the USA and in some of the small streams in northern Italy and Montana. (See also my thoughts on Tenkara, p 97.)

Pocket-waters
Top: Smoky Mountains creek, South Carolina, USA   Above: River Sarca, northern Italy

River Itchen: a classic chalk stream

CHALK STREAMS AND SPRING CREEKS

Chalk streams and spring creeks are at the opposite end of the spectrum from pocket-water and require some significant modification to one's tactical approach. My experience of such waters is limited to the chalk streams and limestone spring creeks of North and East Yorkshire, plus trips to spring creeks in the USA and Slovenia and an occasional trip to the chalk streams in the south of England. However, I'm sure my observations will be relevant to other similar waters.

These waters are a world apart from spate rivers. The key differences are:

- Their water levels do not fluctuate suddenly. Some do show seasonal fluctuations but those with large catchment areas, where the falling rain may take over a year to percolate through the aquifers to the springs, may show little seasonal change in flow rates. As a result, there is often

Foston Beck: a small East Yorkshire chalk stream

limited scouring of the gravel beds which can restrict the availability of good spawning areas. This, in my area, is often further exacerbated by abstraction and siltation from trout farm activity. Secondly, invertebrates and weed-beds have a much more stable habitat within which to flourish, meaning more food and suitable cover for fish.

A further factor that confers habitat stability is that the source water, leaving the aquifers, is a constant temperature (10° C approx in summer and winter).

- In addition, the high pH (alkalinity of the water) and calcium content make for a rich habitat with abundant weed growth (*Ranunculus*, starwort and numerous other species) plus vast numbers of invertebrates (as shown in the table overleaf).

Invertebrates caught kick sampling 1 m² of Driffield West Beck, June 2004

Baetis (olive) nymphs	6370
Blue-winged olive nymphs	202
Simulium (black fly) larvae	3984
Caddis larvae	229
Gammarus (shrimps)	3003
Other organisms	370
TOTAL ORGANISMS	**14158**

- Other than in exceptional circumstances the water is gin clear.
- These rivers are associated with relatively gentle countryside with easy gradients. The habitat is generally structurally uniform with fewer distinctive features (riffles and waterfalls) so the flow is steady with little broken water.

What are the consequences of these differences to the fish and the flyfisher?

- Natural recruitment of trout can be limited: so, unless there is supplementary stocking, trout numbers can be low compared with most spate rivers. Finding suitable targets is, however, aided by the clear water. In my experience, "search-fishing" (casting to likely lies) is generally counter-productive, spooking far too many unnoticed fish. It pays to seek out visible, actively feeding fish (either rising or subsurface feeding) – Polaroid glasses are an essential.

- High, stable populations of food organisms confer rapid growth on piscine inhabitants. It also means that the fish can binge during times when particular species are vulnerable (eg shrimps at night and when an organism is readily available, such as big mayfly exiting their burrows in the riverbed during emergence) followed by long spells of inactivity when they will totally ignore the angler's offerings. Thus, time and thought

Driffield Beck chalk stream, East Yorkshire

must be devoted to considering when might be the best time to be on the river. In early July 2010 I was introducing a novice flyfisher to the popular Mulberry Whin Beat on the Driffield West Beck. We'd fished from 10am till 1pm without success. Over lunch, I explained that the fish were so well-fed due to the super abundance of natural food that they only feed when one or more species of invertebrate is vulnerable but that I expected a brief hatch of small spurwings around mid-afternoon. As predicted, at 2pm the first swallows, martins and swifts were sweeping low over the river in anticipation of the hatch. By 2.30 fish started rising. Within an hour six fish had been landed, four lost and a number missed, all from just one bend in the river, and then the rise switched off as abruptly as it had started. There was no further activity till dusk when a spinner fall prompted half-an-hour of vigorous surface feeding. In favourable conditions feeding may go on all day. In late August 2008 we had vast numbers of black gnats (thanks to the wet summer) and the Mulberry Whin trout fed steadily from 9am till dark. Upwing hatches on my local spring-fed rivers do not coincide with those on the spate streams. During summer on the latter blue-winged olive hatches are generally confined to dusk, whereas on the northern chalk and limestone streams they usually occur from 10am till mid-afternoon. One of my favourite times to fish the Driffield Beck is either side of midday on those baking hot, sunny July or August days when fishing most other waters would be a waste of time. However, in the summer of 2010 things were different: due to very low water conditions (we had little rain between early April and mid-September) daytime fishing was only fair, but during late evening the fish lost their usual caution and fed well on spinners, midges and sedges.

- Clear water and smooth flows make scaring fish a significant potential problem. The usual precautions should be applied *rigorously*. Keep low. Use background or foreground cover. Approach from downstream, if possible. Move very slowly. Avoid false casting if possible. Avoid wading whenever possible. Use long leaders and light lines (I use two- to four-weight rods with one- to three-weight lines and 15 ft plus (5 m plus) leaders. There is little or no "bankside gardening" done on my local waters. As a result, extensive screens of tall reeds provide ideal cover for the angler. A 10 or 11 ft long rod is perfect for reaching over this vegetation and also for handling long leaders. Another invaluable bit of kit is my Vivarelli-style, semi-automatic reel, with which I can instantly collect up any slack-line before

Vivarelli semi-automatic fly-reel

it can become entangled in the bankside jungle, which in turn avoids considerable frustration and dramatically reduces the risk of losing good fish due to loose line coils snagging on vegetation.

- Although the flows are relatively smooth, the extensive weed-beds create a plethora of subtle, sinuous, disturbances on the surface that soon induce drag. In the smooth flows even the slightest micro-drag becomes glaringly obvious, whilst the relatively slow flow rate gives fish plenty of time to detect any flaw in the angler's presentation. Long leaders and long, fine tippet (ideally 5 or 6x, even 7x) combined with appropriate slack-line casts, reach-casts, mends and rod tracking will help delay the onset of significant drag. Should it be impossible to avoid drag (eg when fishing across a weed-bed into a narrow channel) it is worth trying a Sedge or Sedge Pupa imitation since fish learn to expect sedges skittering across the surface and their pupae swimming actively across the flow.

- What about fish location? With a relatively uniform habitat these streams look like one big fish lie. Even with the help of clear water, seeing fish before they see you can be challenging. However, there are obvious places to look for feeding fish that are not actually rising. Brown trout love the margins so pay special attention to the edge of deep undercut banks on the outside of bends, tiny bays in the marginal reeds next to a steady flow/food lane and in front of and behind any overhanging bushes or herbage. Other places to look are in the pocket of calm water immediately in front of a weed-bed and behind gaps in weed-beds where the flow is constricted and drifting food is concentrated. Keep an eye out for clean patches of gravel; some may be where swans have grubbed in the riverbed, but others may be where a fish has swept the gravel clean by its constant tail wafting. Also, on sunny days, look for the shadows of well-camouflaged fish. Whilst trout like to be near to cover, grayling prefer relatively open water where predators and other shoal members can be clearly seen. So,

Big trout lying where food will be channelled to it, Driffield Beck

search them out in the deeper, open pockets between the weed-beds and in weed-free gravel runs.

This then brings us to the choice of flies. I find I need only a small selection to cover all the key spring creek food species.

Upwing hatches are rather inconsistent on some of the waters I fish (a problem on many UK chalk streams according to what I read). I mainly use three patterns, in sizes 14 to 20, to cover all of this group (large dark olives, iron blues, medium olives, pale wateries etc). Mayflies, *Ephemera danica*, have only recently become established in part of Driffield Beck, my local chalk stream. A Paraloop Olive tied with grizzle hackle and a pale buff body is useful when a fly with a bit of weight is needed to cast into a wind, but mostly I use a CdC Gasparin Dun (see p 129) or a CdC IOBO Humpy, whilst a CdC Spent Spinner or Paraloop Pheasant Tail Spinner are useful evening patterns.

SOME THOUGHTS ON TACTICS

Paraloop Olive

Gasparin Dun

IOBO Humpy

Paraloop Pheasant Tail Spinner

Black gnats can be prolific some years, particularly in May with, sometimes, a late summer glut. Hawthorn flies are sometimes important in early May. I tie both with extended micro-chenille bodies, the black gnats on size 20 and size 18 Tiemco 2488, short shank hooks, and the hawthorn flies on size 14s.

Midges are a major food source that most river flyfishers neglect. They are particularly important during dry, low water years. Grayling can become totally preoccupied with the pupae and adults of midges. In May, and again in the late autumn, aphids can be prolific on wooded sections of rivers. On windy days, when they get blown onto the water the fish may become preoccupied with them. An IOBO Humpy in sizes 24 to 30 or a Minimalistic Micro Midge in sizes 26 to 30 will cover these tiny insects and account for a significant percentage of my chalk stream trout.

From mid-May till the end of the trout season a variety of sedges/caddis can be expected, from the tiny (5 mm long) *Agapetus*, in June, to the much larger (2 cm plus) cinnamon sedges of late summer and autumn. A Hackle-less Elk Hair Caddis or F Fly in sizes 20 to 12 covers them all. I don't fuss about colour, since I am sure that size and profile are the key triggers necessary to prompt a take. I should add that in the case of *Agapetus* it is the pupae (actually pharate adults) that are the vulnerable stage when they swim to the riverbank.

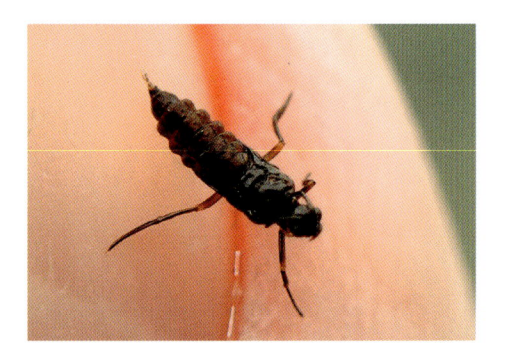

Agapetus fuscipes pupa

Stuart Crofts' artificial Agapetus *pupa*

Craneflies or daddy-long-legs can be seen from April through to the autumn. With declining upwing hatches they are becoming a valuable fly in the chalk stream angler's armoury. They are substantial enough to bring up fish that are only half-heartedly looking up to the surface. If a fish ignores a dead-drifted Daddy then a twitch or two often provides the additional stimulus to trigger a take.

Whilst I much prefer to fish with the dry-fly, there are times when the fish are unprepared to respond even to a Daddy or large Sedge/Caddis. Just three wet-flies cover virtually all my subsurface needs.

Gammarus/freshwater shrimps are prolific in these waters and a

Gammarus pulex

SOME THOUGHTS ON TACTICS

heavily leaded pattern is my first choice, particularly for grayling that can be reticent about surface feeding. I tie them in a range of colours, from natural tan, through subtle pinks and oranges, to garish pink and orange. My favourite, the Ultra Violet Shrimp Pink Shrimp (UVSP Shrimp), is tied with Ultra Violet Shrimp Pink Ice Dub, a subtle orange with a hint of pink and olive.

UVSP Shrimp

Glen Pointon Soft Touch Shrimp

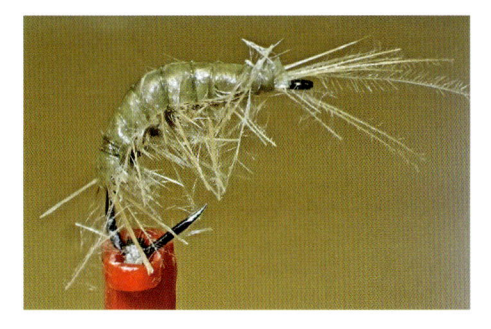

Stuart Crofts' CdC Shrimp

Martin Smith's Shrimps

A Peeping Caddis has accounted for some of my best grayling (up to 3 lb 0 oz) and trout (up to 5 lb 1 oz), proving to be a good fallback fly when the shrimp has failed to interest a fish.

Peeping Caddis

Bead-head Hare's Ear Nymph

Bead-head and Wire Perdigon

Bead-head Hare's Ear Nymphs also have their day. Sometimes the grayling become focused on tiny food items and a size 20 (or smaller) Nymph or Midge Pupa/Buzzer Pupa is all they want. At such times it may be necessary to add some split-shot to the leader to get the tiny fly down (if club rules allow!).

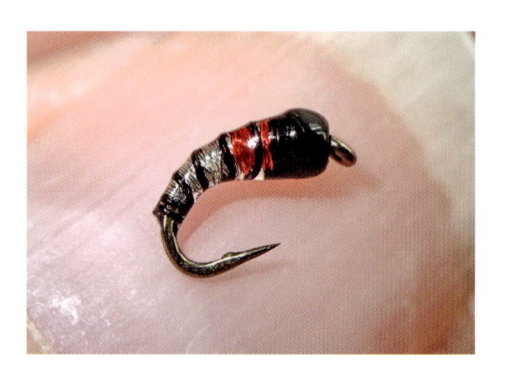

Bead-head and Wire Buzzer Pupa

Finally, can I make a plea for all of you to fight against the insidious destruction of our rivers. Chalk streams and spring creeks in particular are being slowly strangled by abstraction, siltation and pollution. My local Oxfolds/Costa Beck, once one of the country's best fisheries, fished in the past by the likes of Reg Righyni and Eric Horsfall Turner, was totally ruined by over exploitation (water abstraction at its source, two trout farms and a cress bed within the top mile, a sewage outfall near its source and dredging). Hopefully it will eventually recover. Even the lower beats of the prestigious Driffield Beck are just a shadow of their former glory (at its height in the 1960s). Please support bodies like the Wild Trout Trust, the Grayling Society, Wild Fish Conservation, local rivers trusts and the Angling Trust/Fish Legal who are doing their best to protect and restore our waters for future generations.

COPING WITH DROUGHT

The springs and summers of 2010 and 2019 were incredibly dry throughout much of Britain. My area of north-east Yorkshire suffered particularly badly: we had virtually no rain from early April right through till autumn. The small spate streams flowing off the North Yorkshire Moors were down to their bare bones, with virtually no flow. Driffield Beck chalk stream also succumbed to the drought. Consequently, the fishing became progressively harder and harder. One of my close friends, a relative beginner at flyfishing, became more and more frustrated with his rapidly declining ability to tempt fish to a fly. The only consolation I could give him was to say that under such extreme conditions the bar had been raised to a level where normal fishing skills and techniques were insufficient to facilitate the consistent capture of fish.

The problems associated with the drought were as follows:

- The low, clear water caused the wild fish to move out of many of their normal lies in search of cover and a sense of security from predators. Much of the time, when not actively feeding, they were tucked away under the bankside tree roots, deep under overhanging tree branches and beneath the *Ranunculus* beds. When they were in the open they were far spookier than usual, making it much more difficult for the angler to approach his or her quarry.

- High water temperatures and the consequent lowering of the water's oxygen content (due to the lowered solubility of oxygen and the increased oxygen consumption by bacterial breakdown of any organic pollution) made the fish lethargic and less prone to make any effort to take a fly. Their prime concerns were the search for well-oxygenated water and the conservation of what little oxygen their gills could absorb.

- The slow or virtually non-existent flow in many parts of the rivers meant that any feeding fish were often cruising about in search of food, rather

Low water on Driffield Beck

than staying "on station" since most of the "food conveyor belts" had been switched off. This made accurately targeting risers very difficult and increased the chances of "lining" fish and scaring them. It also made search-fishing virtually impossible since a fly cast onto the water did not "search", it just stayed where it had landed.

- The slow flow also gave the fish plenty of time to inspect an angler's fly for any defects of presentation. I lost count of the number of fish that investigated my offerings only to reject them as substandard.

- Some fly hatches were adversely affected, particularly of terrestrials such as black gnats, daddies and hawthorn flies which have larvae that prefer moist conditions. Only on very rare occasions did I find fish "mad on feed" in 2010 and, even then, the windows of opportunity were usually very short, whilst in the spring and summer of 2019 aphids were incredibly abundant and often the rising fish were fixated on them and a size 26 to 30 imitation was required to achieve any significant success.

- Also, tiny midge larvae proliferated in the slow, warm water, resulting in fish which, when in a feeding mood, were often preoccupied with minute pupae, emergers and adults.

So, how can we cope with these challenging conditions? I managed to maintain my catches at decent levels by adapting in a number of crucial ways:

- My approach had to be hyper-stealthy. I wore camouflaged clothing (including hat). Whenever possible I avoided wading. When fishing amongst dense bankside cover I found my semi-automatic reel to be a real godsend since it allowed me to instantly whisk up any loose line before it had a chance to snag up around thistles, bur-reeds and the like. There is nothing more frustrating than finding your line well-entangled with the vegetation whilst trying to cast or, even worse, whilst attempting to give line to a powerful/big fish. If I had no choice but to wade I moved infinitesimally slowly to avoid as far as possible sending ripples and vibrations from the crunching gravel that might alarm the fish. I used any cover I could find. My kneepads got a lot of use since I spent much of my time kneeling down to maintain a low profile and maximise the use of any cover. I also used as long a leader and tippet as was practical (12 to 14 ft on most of the smaller streams and 16 to 18 ft on the larger, more open, chalk streams). This helped to keep the splash of my fly-line as distant as possible and helped to reduce drag. When I had no option but to use a short leader, on the smallest, most overgrown streams, I used a 4 ft long, very delicate, furled leader plus 2 ft of 4x tippet and a further 2 to 3 ft of 6, 7 or 8x tippet. In addition, most of my fishing in 2019 was done with a Sunray Micro Thin one-weight line designed with a 12 ft long, thin front taper for delicate presentation. I also spent inordinate amounts of time just standing, heron-like, so disturbed fish could settle down and start to feed again, only casting when my prey was confidently feeding.

- When search-fishing I concentrated my efforts on those spots where the fish had to be. The fast flows into pool heads, with their well-broken surface providing both cover and plenty of oxygen, were always well-populated with fish, particularly if there was a drop-off into deeper water or the cover provided by tree roots, debris dams, undercut banks and the like close by. It was also much easier to get close to the fish with broken water disrupting the fish's window to the outside world. Furthermore, fish in the fast flow had less time to inspect a fly before committing to take or reject it. It never ceases to amaze me how many fish take up station in the really "skinny water", particularly when oxygen levels are low. Places where a trace of flow passed cover from submerged trees, undercut banks or large boulders, also yielded fish as long as my casting was accurate enough. The extreme conditions really showed up the value of large woody debris (as advocated by the Wild Trout Trust). I regularly fish several neglected sections of river/stream that are so overgrown and full of submerged trees, logs and branches that most club members consider them to be unfishable. They consistently produced fish to my dry-flies even in the most advanced stages of the drought. These well-wooded, tree-shrouded, snag-ridden stretches of stream generally produced better daytime catches than more open reaches, probably because the fish felt less vulnerable to predators, particularly cormorants (which don't like such places).

- When targeting risers that were feeding on station I found I had to cast far more accurately than usual since they were usually reluctant to move far for my fly. Accurate casting also ensured that the fish saw my fly before drag had a chance to set in. When targeting cruisers, I cast only when I was sure where the fish was, either immediately after a rise, when I could predict the fish's direction of travel and speed, or when I could see the fish with the aid of Polaroid sunglasses.

SOME THOUGHTS ON TACTICS

- Despite accurate casting and long leaders with thin, supple tippet, micro-drag was still a serious problem. I found in many instances I had to repeatedly cover a fish (without spooking it) before it would take my offering. This was particularly true when I was using tiny Midges in sizes 24 to 30 since they are much more susceptible to drag than bigger flies. Even dropping down to 8x (0.08 mm) tippet did not completely eliminate this problem. Furthermore, the chalk streams became very weedy by July and even with tiny flies I dared not fish lighter than 6x (0.12 mm) tippet (we didn't weed cut since the weed was the only thing maintaining any semblance of reasonable water levels). During the day most of my fish fell to size 22 and smaller CdC IOBO Humpies. An alternative that worked at times was to use a Daddy or small Elk Hair Caddis, twitching it to alert the fish to the presence of food and induce a take. This also helped to cover water when search-fishing pools with no flow.

- I tend to be lazy and usually attach my flies with a tucked half-blood knot. However, to help reduce micro-drag I used a loop knot (Rapala Knot) much more often than usual, particularly when fishing with tiny midges. This knot allows the fly to pivot independently of the tippet movement. The loop knot is fussier to tie and looks awful when attached to a tiny dry-fly: with two strands of line exiting the hook eye and a relatively big loop clearly visible to the fish you'd think it would scare any half-educated fish. Not so! It definitely increases the number of takes from fussy trout and grayling. My friend Steve commented, after a day's fishing on a desperately low Cumbrian Eden, how obvious was the pivoting back and forth of

Rapala loop knot, 0.10 mm tippet and size 30 CdC midge

his dry-fly attached conventionally and how much less obvious it was when a loop knot was used. We were shown the loop knot by Jesper Larsson, the chief guide at Rajamaa Fish Camp in Sweden, and we are both convinced converts.

- Late evening fishing proved to be well worth the effort. With fading light fish lost some of their caution, moving out from their hideouts under the banks and weed-beds into open water to feed avidly on midges, spent spinners and sedges. At such times I could more easily get close to the fish and could confidently use size 18 and 16 Spinner and Sedge patterns rather than the more usual micro-flies which accounted for most of my daytime catches. Using these larger flies I could, more readily, get away with a trace of micro-drag and use stronger tippets than when fishing with smaller flies.

Finally, I found it necessary to take extra care to ensure that fish which had fought hard in low oxygen situations were carefully revived by holding them facing a good flow for as long as was necessary for them to swim away strongly. (I did not release them as soon as they started to kick, but held them securely till they were kicking vigorously.) I also avoided any waters where the water temperature had become too high and the oxygen level too low, concentrating my efforts on spring-fed streams where the water temperature from the springs remains at 10° C all year round.

All I have written here applies to the wild fish and not stockies. Finding the latter was very simple, they all congregated in the few deep pools, making them highly vulnerable to predators, poachers and anglers alike. Although they became more sluggish they continued to feed right through the brightest, hottest, day and catching them was much easier than catching the wildies. Being habituated to the presence of people they didn't scare easily and being used to regular feeds at the trout farm they didn't go off feed when there was little or no natural food available. I am not a fan of stockies and believe that many waters (those capable of naturally producing good numbers of wild fish)

A cool, spring-fed, limestone brook, North Yorkshire

would benefit dramatically from a drastic reduction of, or even cessation of, stocking. Despite this I must confess that stockies did give many anglers some chance of catching a fish or two under very challenging conditions and they did allow me to give a few friends trout to eat without my having to deplete the wild stocks (I never kill wild fish).

FISHING IN THE COLD

Many flyfishers avoid really cold conditions. Some of my friends completely stop fishing when the brown trout season ends at the end of September and don't start again till the season opens again in March or April. Yet there is some superb flyfishing to be had during the coldest parts of the year. Furthermore, severe cold can occur even during the trout season.

Most folks associate grayling with winter fishing and they are undoubtedly

Winter Tenkara, Yorkshire Derwent

an ideal target species since they positively thrive in cold waters and will feed in the coldest of conditions. As winter progresses the grayling in my local streams tend to move into the deeper and slower parts of the river, where they become far more reticent to rise to a dry-fly or even move up in the water for a nymph or shrimp pattern. Deep-fished flies become the order of the day, teamed up with a Tenkara or a very long, light, conventional rod combined with super light lines/leaders and a semi-curly bicolour indicator between line/leader and tippet. I like to fish at close range with all the line/leader and the indicator held above the river surface, whilst tracking the rod to keep in touch with my fly/flies trundling along the riverbed. By keeping the thicker line/leader off the fast surface flow it is possible to present the fly/flies as near as possible at the flow rate near the riverbed; at the same time keeping everything taut between indicator and fly/flies ensures that takes are instantly indicated. The big advantages of Tenkara are:

SOME THOUGHTS ON TACTICS

- There are no rod rings to freeze up.

- There is no need to handle cold, wet fly-line.

- Gloves can be worn.

- It is even possible to keep the non-rod hand in a warm pocket.

- The rods are very long and so are ideal for Czech-nymphing.

Cold conditions do not mean that there is no prospect of dry-fly fishing. My first experience of the excellent dry-fly fishing that can be had in adverse conditions was many years ago on my local Yorkshire Derwent. It was early April, supposedly spring! I was hoping for a hatch of large dark olives. Arriving at the river at 11am conditions seemed less than ideal with a chilly 4°C temperature after an overnight frost, and there was heavy cloud cover. An hour passed with little sign of fish, just an isolated trout that fell to a Nymph. Then at noon the snow started to fall in huge flakes. As the snowstorm intensified I noticed the first small dark grey "yacht" drifting down a current seam at the head of one of my favourite pools, soon to be followed by a few more and then a flotilla of them – large dark olive duns. This brought on one of the best spells of dry-fly fishing that I've experienced so early in the season. The water temperature was a reasonable 8°C but, on reaching the cold surface air, the LDO (large dark olive) duns did not have the energy to lift off into the air. They were trapped on the surface, easy prey for the eager trout.

Later on that spring, in early May, I made the 45-minute yomp deep into the upper water of the Yorkshire Derwent. I had just caught my first wild brown trout on a Peeping Caddis when the sun disappeared and the hailstorm of all hailstorms started. For well over half an hour I cowered under a big conifer watching the scene turn from brown and green to white. The river surface was totally covered with hailstones and the water temperature had dropped from 8°C to 4°C. Furthermore, the meltwater was turning the river brown. Surely my fishing was over… As I trudged dejectedly back towards my car, the returning sun was causing water to drip from the overhanging trees into the river. I noticed one drip that looked like a swirl. Surely it couldn't be a rising fish? There were a few black gnats in the air so I attached a size 18 imitation to the end of my tippet and covered the spot. Much to my surprise a fish rose and a small wild trout was landed. The next surprise was that I noticed assorted flies hatching, iron blues, olive uprights and even a couple of early mayflies, followed by more rising fish. On that return journey to the car I caught another sixteen trout on an assortment of dry-flies.

On my local small stillwater, Wansford Lake, near Driffield, East Yorkshire, some of the best dry-fly fishing of the year is to be had on the frostiest, snowiest days of winter. The lake is fed from the local chalk stream system and so never freezes over. Furthermore, it has a distinct flow, being a U-shaped canal with both inlet and outlet. Midges emerge all year long: mainly in the low light conditions of early mornings, late evenings and dull days. As with the LDOs, cold, dull days provide perfect fishing conditions because yet again the emerging adults are too cold to take to the air and so linger on the surface in huge numbers, particularly in areas where wind and current concentrate them. At such times "wolf packs" of stocked rainbow trout and occasional wild brown trout rise like clockwork to the abundance of readily available food. In the cold winter of 2017/18 I had amazing dry-fly fishing with size 24 to 30 CdC Midges just after dawn on the frostiest of mornings and again around sunset. On one particular day, during the "Beast From The East!" storm, when sunny spells were interspersed with heavy snow showers, it was noticeable that the midges were only emerging in the lower light during snow squalls and this was the only time that I caught fish. The lower water temperatures of winter also slow down the ascent of the midge pupae, so even if the fish are not feeding on the surface a tiny Buzzer Pupa suspended from a small dry-fly, greased semi-curly bicolour indicator or greased leader will usually tempt plenty of fish.

Winter at Wansford Lake, East Yorkshire

September conditions, Krimmler Ache, Austria

One of my most surreal experiences of dry-fly fishing in severe cold was in September 2012 when Stu Crofts, Steve Donohue, Don Stazicker and I had a couple of days' fishing on the upper Krimmler Ache, above the Krimml Falls in Austria, at a height of over 5000 ft above sea level. Our first day, when we caught loads of fish: brown trout, brook trout and grayling on dry-flies, was cool and dull, with a bit of drizzle. That evening it started to snow heavily and the following morning the thermometer outside the alpine hut, where we were staying, registered -6° C. Whilst wading through the deep snow, heading for the river upstream of the hut, my friends told me that I had to catch the first fish of the day on a floating black beetle, Le Scarab Noire. This had become a daily tradition after I had been greeted as "Monsieur Le Scarab Noire" earlier on this trip by a French angler, a nickname that related to an incident several years previous when using a Black Foam Beetle I'd caught several big rainbow from a pool where he had blanked. In such cold conditions, with the snow still falling, I was anything but confident about my ability to catch anything on a floating fly. Nevertheless, I headed for a small shallow pool on a side stream that I knew was full of small brook trout and, much to the surprise of all, first cast I caught a baby brookie. Thus started the most amazing day, when all of us caught good numbers of brown trout and brook trout fishing with Foam Beetles and dry caddis fly patterns. The trick on the day was to land a bulky fly, with a plop, in the narrow zone of nearly static water between the turbulent main flow and the marginal rocks. Thanks to the use of long Tenkara rods and super-light, level nylon lines we were able to hold all our line off the fast water, facilitating a perfect drag-free drift in the narrow band of slow water along the rock edges from beneath which the fish would slowly appear to leisurely "yawn-in" our dry-flies.

Don't forget that there are also pike and perch to be caught in the depths of winter, although the warmer conditions of autumn and early March are undoubtedly the best times for these species which are more adversely affected by very low water temperatures than are grayling.

So, don't let the cold stop you from enjoying your flyfishing. Get well wrapped up and make the most of the opportunities that these conditions can provide.

PERSISTING

I've mentioned earlier how critical it can be to avoid even micro-drag when fishing the dry-fly and how, when fishing subsurface flies, sometimes the fish want an absolutely dead-drifted offering, whilst at other times a subtle lift at the right time will induce a take from an apparently indifferent fish.

Achieving a perfect presentation is easier said than done. I hate to think how many times I've watched a fish reject my fly despite my best efforts, usually because of poor presentation. To attain a drag-free drift with the dry-fly we might use a number of strategies (often a combination of several), including: parachute-casts, reach-casts, mends, extra-long leaders, supple materials such as furled leaders and fine copolymer tippet, rod-tracking and feeding loose line. Even with these and other tactics it is probable that we never achieve a truly drag-free drift. Micro-drag is a virtually ever-present problem. The behaviour of any fly attached to tippet will be affected to some degree by the action of water currents on the tippet. This is particularly true when using small flies, which have less inertia to resist movement and less surface area to form hydrophilic (water-loving) bonds with the water molecules near it. When floatant is applied to dry-flies, or if using CdC flies, which are hydrophobic (water-repelling), then there are no forces binding the fly to the particular nuance of current on which it is resting. Part of the success of emergers, with submerged bodies, is undoubtedly their resistance (be it ever so slight) to drag from the action of currents on the tippet. I could go into a lot of technical jargon about hydrogen bonding and the combined strength of vast numbers of weak hydrogen bonds, but I suspect relatively few would be interested in the technicalities. Suffice it to say that there are genuine scientific reasons why the submerged bodies of flies such as Klinkhåmers help to resist drag.

At least when fishing to rising fish we know with a fair degree of certainty where our quarry is, so accurate casting and reducing/delaying drag are the only presentational problems we face (as long as we haven't scared the fish). When fishing using the "induced take" with wet-flies, unless we are fortunate enough to be able to sight fish on a clear chalk stream, timing the lift is a matter of pure chance. Even when we are sight fishing it may be difficult to determine the precise location of our Nymph/Shrimp/Bug, making accurate timing of the induced lift problematical.

How can we overcome these difficulties? At one time I was firmly of the opinion that the first cast was critical and that thereafter the chance of tempting the fish was inversely proportional to the number of casts made. I no longer believe this to be always the case. Numerous observations to the contrary have led me to believe that there are many times when the opposite is true. As long as I have managed to avoid scaring my quarry I will repeatedly cast to a fish until, by a combination of appropriate tactics and pure chance, hopefully, I achieve the perfect presentation and the fish is fooled. Occasionally a fish's early refusals to take my fly have been because I'd chosen a fly with the wrong triggers (too big, wrong profile, wrong colour), but more often it has been because my presentation has not been quite right. Regularly, when I am having success other anglers ask, "What fly are you using?" They never ask, "How are you presenting your fly?" Sure, the choice of fly is important; it's usually no good offering a size 12 Sedge to a grayling that is rising to tiny midge pupae, but precise presentation is critical. This is particularly true for grayling on the dry-fly; I find them to be much fussier about micro-drag than trout. However, it also applies to well-educated trout in heavily fished waters, where they have learned to avoid any fly that behaves unnaturally. On my 2009 trip to Soda Butte Creek in Yellowstone National Park, Wyoming, I even saw well-educated cutthroat trout inspect and reject natural insects that were being buffeted by the wind. These fish were quite unconcerned by the close proximity of anglers, but had become conditioned to the fact that unnaturally behaving flies resulted in an unpleasant experience. Only by repeatedly covering each of these fish was an adequate presentation finally achieved and the fish caught.

Let me relate several other examples that support my opinions that persistence can pay dividends…

CASE 1: Late August 2008, Pickering Beck, North Yorkshire

A grayling was rising in the margins about ten metres above me. It was obviously feeding on tiny midges so I tied a size 24 CdC IOBO Humpy onto my 14 ft leader ending in 7x tippet. For several reasons, my only practical angle of approach was from directly downstream. My first cast landed perfectly (or so I thought), the fly landing delicately just above my target, with plenty of slack to cope with any possible drag: but no! The vagaries of the current immediately caused my fly to drag very slightly across the flow (so slightly that if I had not been fishing at very close range, and if there hadn't been a few bubbles on the surface close to it, I'd never have noticed my fly's deviant movements). My offering was ignored. Five or six more casts ended up with the same scenario. Meanwhile the fish continued to rise to naturals. After another half-dozen casts I produced one where I could discern no micro-drag and the fish rose with confidence. My reward for such persistence was a nice 32 cm grayling.

CASE 2: Late September 2008, Driffield Beck

A sizeable grayling was clearly visible over a patch of marginal gravel in about four feet of fast water. It took about a dozen casts to tempt what proved to be a 2 lb 15 oz fish to take my heavily weighted Peeping Caddis. Why didn't it take during one of the previous casts? I'm sure that it was because the presentation just hadn't been quite right.

CASE 3: Late October 2008, Yorkshire Derwent

Whilst working up a very shallow glide, a fish rose just above me; so close that my 12 ft leader was all I needed outside the rod tip. I was sure it was a grayling and equally sure it was feeding on the tiny aphids that were being dislodged in good numbers from the falling autumn leaves. I tied on a size 26 CdC IOBO Humpy and covered the fish. It made no response despite an apparently perfect drift! It continued to rise confidently; several times rising within an inch of my fly. Nevertheless, repeated casting was to no avail. I moved my attention to another fish rising a bit further up, which proved to be a small wild brownie. The first fish was still rising intermittently, so I returned my attention to it. Finally, after over

30 casts, a grayling of 30 cm succumbed to my offering. I'm convinced that the earlier refusals were due to a combination of micro-drag in some instances and the distraction of the abundant naturals in others.

CASE 4: Mid-September 2009, Lamar River, Yellowstone National Park

A good-sized cutthroat trout was regularly rising just above a large, submerged boulder, which was creating a plethora of complex currents. An approach from upstream was impractical, since there were two other good fish feeding above my target and I didn't want to spook them. My only option was to cast my size 20 CdC Emerger across the awkward currents, putting plenty of slack into the line/leader and hope for the best. A dozen casts failed to induce a take, although she came and looked at the fly once. She finally stopped rising – put down by a careless cast? A five-minute wait and she was rising again. Another couple of minutes to let her get back into a confident feeding rhythm and I resumed my assault. It took another half-dozen or so casts to finally get a good drift and hook that fish, a beautiful 18½ in female cutthroat.

CASE 5: February 17, 2010, Wansford Lake, nr Driffield, East Yorkshire

Wansford Lake is a U-shaped "canal" with a distinct flow. Wansford fish see a lot of anglers, most of whom fish catch-and-release. As a result, the fish very soon wise up, becoming extremely challenging. Furthermore, the primary food source is micro-buzzer pupae which drift with the flow, rising and sinking imperceptibly slowly. One of the most successful tactics therefore is to fish a tiny buzzer (size 24 or smaller) suspended a foot or two under a small dry-fly or from a well-greased leader. When the water is clear it is possible to watch the fish's reactions to the fly. Often, they will take the Buzzer on the drop but only if it is sinking with and not across the flow. To achieve this the tippet between the dry-fly and buzzer must land parallel to the flow, which can be facilitated by a cast directly upstream, using a dump/parachute-cast, or by kicking a right angle in the leader during an across-stream cast. At other times takes come during the drift, which must be exactly at the pace of the subsurface flow. When choosing a fishing spot, I don't necessarily pick the site where the most fish are. I find a spot where the surface drift and subsurface flow are the same. I do this by throwing a small ball of soaked paper tissue into the water next to a bit of floating debris or bubbles so that I can check that they drift at the same rate. Despite these attempts to achieve a perfect presentation I get many rejections and repeated casting to targeted fish is usually necessary for any semblance of consistent success. On the day in question there was a steady hatch of micro-buzzers and about a dozen rainbows were rising sporadically to the adults, which looked like specks of soot on the surface. I tied a size 26 CdC IOBO Humpy onto the end of an 18 ft long leader to 6x tippet (the lightest I dared to use since some of the risers were fish of around 6 lb). It took me two hours and countless casts to tempt just six of those fish (only four landed). Literally hundreds of times I had fish come and inspect my offering, only to reject it because of micro-drag. Only when I got things just right did a fish finally commit itself.

Rainbow trout and size 30 Wire Buzzer

CASE 6: June 5, 2010, Driffield Beck

It was a warm, dull evening. I'd just caught a couple of good brown trout when I saw my friend John further upstream. Enquiring of his success he said he'd had one but had been unsuccessfully targeting a big brown trout that was still rising steadily. He kindly invited me to have a go for it. First cast my size 18 Elk Hair Caddis drifted perfectly. The fish rose and, in my excitement, I whipped the fly out of its mouth, pricking him in the process. Chance blown! I thought so, but within a couple of minutes the trout was rising confidently again. I covered it a few times, more in hope than expectation. Then, after probably a dozen or more casts (with rests between to make sure it was still feeding on naturals), I got a perfect drift. It rose. This time I hooked it and after a dogged fight John netted it for me, 23½ in and an

5 lb Driffield Beck brown trout

estimated 5 lb. Thanks, John, for your generosity in giving me the chance to catch such a fine fish...

Under challenging conditions achieving precise presentation or a sufficiently accurate cast, even one cast in five, may be difficult for mere mortals like me. In other situations, it might be the sheer abundance of natural food forms that reduces the chance of a fish taking the artificial as it passes by. Whatever the reason for my fly being rejected, I'll continue to *try, try and try again* till either I spook the fish, get bored with trying or (hopefully) tempt my prey.

TRIALS WITH TENKARA

By now you'll know I believe that when it comes to catching trout and grayling presentation is nine-tenths of the game. It was early in 2010 that I first read about Tenkara in *Fly Fishing and Fly Tying* magazine but, although finding it interesting, I dismissed the technique as irrelevant to my fishing. However, in autumn 2010 a friend asked what I knew about the method, which was virtually zero! Checking on the Internet, I discovered a style of fishing which focuses nearly exclusively on presentation.

This traditional Japanese method, believed to date back to the 9thC BC, uses a long rod (11 to 15 ft), with a very delicate line (furled horsehair of about 11 ft or longer) attached to the tip, plus a 5 to 7x tippet of about 2 to 6 ft. It evolved as a very efficient method for the capture of the small native salmonids from the mountain streams of Japan. It is said that, on such waters, a good Tenkara fisher can out-fish an angler using modern techniques 5:1. The method is so efficient that commercial Japanese fishermen used it. Traditionally the line was furled horsehair, whilst the rods were bamboo. In the UK Charles Cotton used a long rod and fixed horse hair line in the late 1600s, whilst in northern Italy the ancient style of Valsesiana fishing with a long rod, fixed line and team of spider-style wet-flies is still employed by a

Modern Tenkara rods

few anglers. Modern Tenkara rods are made from carbon fibre, weigh a mere 2½ to 3½ oz, are telescopic and pack down to just 20 in long. Rod actions are very soft in the tip and are graded, 5:5, 6:4, 7:3 and 8:2. 5:5 rods are soft, slow actioned in which the top 50 per cent of the rod bends easily, whilst 8:2 rods are fast, tip-actioned, and only the top 20 per cent bends easily. Modern lines are synthetic materials (copolymer or fluorocarbon) from 7 to 15 ft and even longer, and may be tapered or level. A short, soft, braid loop or a slipknot is used to attach the leader/line to the braid (Lilian String) permanently attached to the rod tip. Lines are very light; typically, level lines are 8 to 12 lb (approximately 0.285 mm diameter) fluorocarbon, which facilitates extra-delicate presentation. Hi-vis, bright yellow or orange lines help detect subtle takes when fishing subsurface: alternatively, a short section of hi-vis braid or coiled hi-vis 15 lb copolymer can be attached between leader and tippet.

Tenkara is certainly an ideal way of presenting flies in the typical pocket-

Tenkara, Filzbach, Austria

water of mountain streams. Earlier I mentioned the use of high-sticking with a 10 ft rod, 12 ft leader and virtually no fly-line out of the rod tip: well, Tenkara is even better suited to this style of close combat fishing. The longer rod makes several things easier: reaching over conflicting flows to avoid drag, casting the fly precisely into any seam or small pocket of calmer water, then holding virtually all the line/tippet off the water whilst tracking with the rod so that no drag occurs when fishing with dry-flies. Line/tippet combinations much longer than the rod hinder holding most of the line off the water (1 to 2 ft longer than the rod is in my opinion about ideal).

As for other methods of presentation, the induced take, á là Frank Sawyer/Oliver Kite, can be very precisely controlled using a short, tight line unimpeded by drag from wayward flows or the buffering effect of a heavy conventional fly-line. In addition, using soft hackle wet-flies, nymphs and bugs with this method allows the fly to be given tiny, controlled, lifts so that the fly pulses with simulated life (very similar to the way that some pole-fishers

Tenkara, Hollersbach, Austria

constantly lift and drop their bait so it sinks naturally in order to entice a take from roach and other coarse fish). Traditional Tenkara, Reversed Kebari wet-flies are similar to our traditional spiders and the Italian Valsesia flies. Both Kebari and Valsesia flies are tied more heavily dressed than North Country Spiders, often with the hackle reversed so the fibres slope over the hook eye (like Neil Patterson's Funnel Dun). This reversed hackle facilitates the maximum movement of the hackle fibres when the fly is worked by the current or by repeated, subtle lifts of the rod tip. Another, interesting Tenkara technique for tempting fish is Sutebari (which means "throw away the fly") where the fly is "quick-fire" cast in an arc, close to the fish,

Woodcock and Orange Sakasa Kebari

never letting it settle more than a second or two on the water and then the final cast is made to the sweet spot directly in front of the target, which if suitably excited will take without hesitation.

Presentation is much more important than fly choice and Tenkara patterns are suggestive rather than imitative. Apparently some Tenkara fishers use only one fly-pattern all year round. Presentation may be nine-tenths of the game but,

Austrian brook trout

as Dick Walker used to say, "You can't catch nine-tenths of a fish," so unless your fly is appropriate for the particular fishing situation you won't catch. I certainly would not restrict myself to such a limited range of flies. I could not imagine not using my size 24 and smaller CdC dries, or small bead-head nymphs and shrimps. A melding of traditional Tenkara with modern techniques is the way I have gone. Just as modern materials have improved on the old in the construction of Tenkara equipment, so techniques can be evolved and adapted. Versatility, plus an open mind, is the best recipe for consistent success.

Casting with a Tenkara set-up is not dissimilar to casting using a conventional outfit with a few key differences. Firstly, there is no line to shoot so the left hand is obsolete (except for the final landing of a fish). The standard hand grip is with the forefinger extended along the top of the handle which facilitates precise, accurate casting and the casting stroke is generally a short 10 to 12 o'clock, 12 to 10 o'clock sequence, with stops to allow the line to extend fully (too sharp a stop causes recoil vibrations from the soft top). Roll casts and oval casts are easily performed and under arm oval casts are great for casting under overhanging branches. The latter cast is very similar to a tennis player sweeping up a low ball, whilst in very tight spots a bow and arrow cast can be easily executed thanks to the flexibility of these rods

Having purchased a 12 ft, Tenkara USA, Iwana, 6:4 rod just as the November 2010 blizzards hit East Yorkshire, my first chance to try it out was not until the 5th of December, when daytime temperatures rose to an elevated 2°C and local roads became passable. I headed for the upper Yorkshire Derwent, which was clear despite some meltwater. On arrival I carefully hitched my 10½ ft furled leader/line to the braid tag (Lilian) attached to the rod tip, then extended the eight telescopic sections, after which I added 5 ft of 6x (0.12 mm) tippet, with a tiny pinch of pink float dough at its junction with the leader, plus a size 14 UV Shrimp Pink Ice Dub Shrimp at the terminal end. At less than 3 oz the rod felt like a wand and a slight flick pitched my offering into the head of the nearside seam in a pool that nearly always holds grayling. First cast and the leader tip pulled away after drifting about a metre. A lively 25 cm brown trout quickly came to hand. In the following hour and a half, three similar sized grayling were landed and another three dropped off. I learnt several things on that first day: casting was very easy and very accurate, but, having a fixed line length, I had to make sure I positioned myself carefully to cover each potential lie/holding spot: tracking with the rod held at 45° was essential to ensure a drag-free drift and to keep in close contact with the fly.

My second trial was on the 7th of December. The sub-zero temperature was no problem, with no rod rings to freeze up. Also, with no reel or manual line manipulation required I could wear my mittens, only needing to fold back the ends of one when unhooking a fish. A slightly shorter leader set up, consisting of a 7 ft furled leader with 1 ft of bright yellow braid attached and 5 ft of tippet proved to be perfect, allowing me to track the rod with the flow whilst holding the yellow braid just above the water surface. Casting up and across the flow facilitated good presentation. In less than two hours seven grayling up to 30 cm, and a 46 cm brown trout, fell for the charms of my Pink Shrimp.

Winter Tenkara, Yorkshire Derwent

The shorter line made playing the fish straightforward and I was particularly impressed with how well the set-up handled the sizeable brown trout: the soft action of the rod and stretch in the furled leader just soaked up the fish's power. Subsequent winter trips, with temperatures down to -7°C, convinced me how effective a Tenkara set-up is for nymphing/bugging. Roll on April and the dry-fly fishing.

Tenkara has really taken off in the USA, with anglers like Ed Engle, John Gierach and Yvon Chouinard extolling the advantages of this simple method and it has developed a sizeable following in the UK. It is certainly an ideal means of introducing youngsters and beginners to flyfishing on rivers since casting and line management are relatively easy and it is a brilliant way of presenting flies. Its only drawbacks are that it is not ideally suited to the catching of large fish, such as the oversized stockies that are so often introduced into our rivers to compensate for poor spawning habitat, over-fishing or to satisfy the desire of anglers who want big fish that are easy to catch; it is also unsuitable for heavily overgrown, tree-enshrouded small streams and the very light line is easily affected by the wind. Furthermore, the ultra-light tip is not suited to the use of large, thick-wired hooks. On the other hand, Tenkara is very well-suited to fishing with small weighted nymphs and bugs, spiders and dry-flies. Although it will never take over from my more conventional equipment, I've had great fun with it and will continue to use it in the right places and at the right times. As I've said earlier: variety is the spice of life. If you haven't tried it why not give Tenkara a try? If you do, remember that you will be working at very close range so absolute stealth is paramount, particularly with trout which usually tend to spook more easily than grayling.

ITALIAN STYLE CASTING

Having realized the significant advantages Tenkara offers for facilitating drag-free drifts, and for creating subtle movements to animate nymphs, bugs and some dry-flies to induce a take from trout and grayling, I now regularly fish Tenkara – particularly on tumbling pocket-waters where it confers major advantages. However, there are situations when Tenkara is inappropriate, for example very windy days or when the fish cannot be approached close enough, or where the fish are too big to handle on a fixed line and 5x tippet (the heaviest that should be used with most Tenkara rods).

There are two very effective alternatives that go some way to offering Tenkara's quality of presentation. The first, Leader to Hand/Euro-nymphing/French Nymphing, has been well publicised. With its long, light rods and long, light leaders it comes close to Tenkara, but like all methods it has its limitations. It can be difficult in really windy conditions and it can be a challenge to cast a fly any distance under low, overhanging trees. The second, Italian Style casting, works well when fishing with dry-flies in windy conditions and on rivers that are heavily tree-lined. Fortunately for me, my

Massimo Magliocco casting Italian Style

good friend Manu Gonetto (who is part of the Fly Fishing Masters [FFM] UK Italian Casting team) showed me the style when we fished together on the Yorkshire Derwent. It gave us a chance to compare the presentation possible with this style with that of Tenkara. Although Tenkara offered a better chance of drag-free drifts I was impressed by the quality of drifts achieved with the Italian Style compared with the more conventional UK style of casting. Having had my interest aroused, in the summer of 2013 I attended a weekend-course near Derby, run by top Italian caster Massimo Magliocco, which further convinced me of the value of learning this innovative style and where I gained some of the basic skills required.

My first practical trials with the technique were carried out on my local small stillwater where there are complex flows at the inlet and where very accurate casting with tiny dry-flies (size 26 to 30) is required if consistent success is to be achieved with the hyper-educated, midge-feeding rainbows. I teamed up an 8 ft fast-actioned, two/three-weight rod with a one-weight DT line, 12 ft tapered leader and 4 ft of 7x tippet. I was amazed at the effectiveness of my less than perfect performance. Even into a brisk breeze my line and leader were shooting out with incredible accuracy, generally with a fly-first landing and little disturbance from the landing leader and line. Furthermore, I was getting several seconds of drag-free drift and the result was a good number of fooled rainbows.

In the late summer of 2013 my local north-east Yorkshire streams were desperately low and clear, with virtually no flow. Only a few of the pool heads had enough broken water to facilitate a close enough approach for Tenkara. Due to the spooky nature of the fish in these extreme conditions, in most places long casts were essential. Many of the fish were located in the thin pool tails or tight under overhanging trees, both of which offered real challenges; the first with regard to spooking the fish, plus the avoidance of drag (as the line had to be cast over the faster riffle below the pool tail) and the second with the need for accurate casting into very tight spaces. The Italian style seemed an appropriate answer to these problems. Arriving at 10am on a bright, hot, sunny, late August day I found the Derwent lower and clearer than I'd ever seen it in any of the previous 13 years. Two members that I met were complaining of the dour fishing, with few risers and most of them in impossible spots tight against the banks under the trees. Once again, the Italian Style proved its efficacy. Although not easy fishing, I steadily picked up fish to a size 20 Shuttlecock. The hyper-tight loops and accurate casting allowed me to reach fish in spots I would have found very difficult in the past, whilst the extra seconds of drag-free drift (compared with my normal casting techniques, including reach-casts and dump-casts) helped considerably. The only real problem I encountered was that I dropped off a fair number of fish due to the inefficiencies of fishing at long range with plenty of slack and a short rod. I had several other subsequent visits with progressively deteriorating water levels and, on all occasions, I caught far more fish than I expected to.

So, what are the main features and – more importantly – what are the real advantages of this method?

- There is a much-extended rod stroke in which the normal power snap (thrust) is followed by a purposeful "drift" (vibration dampening), allowing for a continuous casting action which, when coupled with precise rod-tracking, generates very high line speed and incredibly tight loops (not suitable for weighted nymphs!). This facilitates the use of light lines. Furthermore, it makes accurate casting into the wind or casting deep under overhanging trees much easier.
- In most casts the fly lands first, then the leader, and finally the line, thus drag induced by the action of currents on the leader and line is significantly delayed. Furthermore, trout target the first object that hits the water near to them. If that is the fly rather than the leader or line then the fish is far less likely to be spooked or to ignore the fly. This is very similar to Tenkara.
- Many of the casts are designed to introduce controlled amounts of slack to delay drag.
- Due to the high line speed and tight loops generated, a short, fast action rod is teamed up with a DT line one or even two weights lighter than would be used for conventional casting. Fishing with such light set-ups can become addictive.
- A long, articulated, hand-built, tapered leader – in which each section is joined with tiny perfection loops – further limits the effects of drag. (I've been using a standard 12 ft tapered leader plus 4 ft of tippet.)
- A unique "wrap-around" grip that helps with precise rod control.

In the autumn of 2013, I had the great fortune to be invited over to Italy to take part in one of FFM Italy's casting courses with the possibility that I might become an instructor for FFM UK. This took place over four days in late November at Ascoli (a 2½ hour drive west of Rome). The hospitality of Massimo and the other Italians was unbelievable, as was the high standard of their casting (not to mention the local food and wine!). Each day involved casting instruction and demonstrations, practicing the casts with feedback from the instructors, the recording on video of each participant, followed by group discussions of each person's strengths and weaknesses and how to resolve any problems, plus an evening theory session and social activities such as fly-tying.

4 lb 14 oz trout caught during a gale, thanks to the Italian Style of casting

My biggest trout of 2017, a wild fish of 4 lb 14 oz from Driffield Beck, was caught on a size 20 dry-fly (*Agapetus* Pupa) on a day when the wind was gusting at 45 mph and my only chance of accurately covering the fish was with my Italian Casting set-up and Italian Casting style.

Massimo and his team are constantly working on improving the dynamics of many of the casts, so this is not a fossilized, inflexible style but one that is evolving with time to further enhance the presentation of dry-flies.

This elegant style not only looks impressive but is impressive in the way it delivers dry-flies accurately into apparently impossible places and in its capacity to achieve drag-free drifts, plus its ability to deliver a light line and long leader into the wind. It is therefore well worth the effort of learning. Furthermore, these short rod and light lines are very enjoyable to fish with. If you fish dry-flies on rivers, give it a try: I'm sure that you will be impressed. It is also worth mentioning that it works well with very small nymphs either with a fly-line or a French leader. Although a short, custom-designed rod is the ideal for this technique it will also work with longer rods, and I often use the style with a 10 ft two-weight rod with either a one-weight line or micro-nymph line.

FLOATANTS

Floatants are an essential part of every flyfisher's armoury, but from what I see on the river and lake banks many folks do not seem to make optimum use of them. The first thing I do before any fishing session is to apply suitable floatants to my line, leader and, when appropriate, to my fly. I should point out that I am talking about floating lines and leaders (I very rarely use sinking lines for the rivers and small stillwaters that I fish). I virtually never see other anglers grease up their line and leader before fishing, yet I consider it to be absolutely essential. Why?

A high-floating line with a hydrophobic (water-hating) coating will lift off the water more easily and more smoothly. This confers several distinct advantages. It causes less fish-scaring disturbance when lifting off to recast or when striking into a fish. Less energy is required when striking into a fish, resulting in a dramatically improved chance of hooking the fish. Mending the line to control drag is far easier and causes less disturbance. Finally, the line is far less likely to be dragged under the surface by down-welling currents that can lead to a snagged line and problems when trying to strike into fish.

The same applies to greasing the leader. Furthermore, a greased leader can be used as an indicator of takes when nymph fishing. In the old days before "bungs", New Zealand wool, bicolour mono and bright braid indicators were developed, we used to just watch a well-greased leader as it drifted on the river or lake surface to signal any takes whilst fishing nymphs or buzzers. I still use this method when I'm fishing buzzers on the drop on smooth lake surfaces. I just watch the greased part of the leader where it sinks through the surface film and strike at any change in sink rate. Recently, with the appearance on

A range of floatants and sinkants

the market of fluorescent pink, orange, white, red and yellow greases and waxes, some folks are turning back to watching a greased leader for takes. It is far more subtle than buoyant float dough or a bung and even quicker to apply and remove than a New Zealand wool indicator or my favorite semi-curly, bicolour mono indicator.

When applying grease to my dry-fly leaders I apply it to within 2 in/5 cm of my fly; this ensures that when I lift off to recast my fly (often a CdC fly) is not pulled under the water surface, which can scare the fish and waterlog the fly. This ensures that no false casting is required before recasting to the target fish. I avoid false casting as much as possible. All too often I see anglers looking more like metronomes than flyfishers and sometimes it is possible to see the fish fleeing when they see their lines repeatedly flying through the air. It also ensures that I do not have to waste time drying and regreasing my dry-fly. I must confess to never using degreaser when fishing dry-flies as I find it to be relatively ineffective at sinking fine copolymer tippet and I hate fluorocarbon because it is too stiff, too costly and, most importantly, does not degrade in sunlight if left hanging from a snag which can make it a long-term risk to wildlife. Some folks say that I am an idiot

Neon wax applied to the leader, or copolymer curly indicator, aids floatation and visibility

because a floating tippet will put the fish off, but I haven't found this to be the case and I know that Stuart Crofts, a more experienced flyfisher than I am, doesn't bother degreasing his dry-fly tippet either. If you've ever used buoyant putty as an indicator on the 0.55 mm diameter (30 lb breaking strain) butt of a tapered leader, you'll know how many fish rise to and take hold of the blob of putty: now I ask you, "Surely the fish could clearly see the floating, thick leader butt, yet they still take the putty thinking it is food?" So why bother using fluorocarbon or degreasing to sink the tippet?

However, grease can be a problem when fishing with nymphs. Whilst a well-greased line and leader butt, plus where appropriate a greased indicator, is in my opinion essential, grease on the tippet will seriously hinder sinking when we want a fly to sink quickly, for example when grayling fishing in winter. I only want grease on my nymphing tippet if I want a fly to sink slowly or to be suspended just below the surface film. A degreaser, such as Fuller's Earth mixed with washing-up liquid and glycerine, or Hunt's Original Mud, is very useful for removing any grease from the tippet during nymph fishing.

The application of grease/floatant to a floating line is particularly important if you are using a line that is denser than water, a silk line or a Sunray Micro Thin line, since these lines float thanks to the hydrophobic coating of grease repelling water molecules and stop the line breaking through the surface tension. (Sunray Micro Thin lines have a hydrophobic plastic coating but any dirt sticking to this can affect its floatability so greasing certainly helps.)

So, what about dry-flies? I have tried out a wide range of silicone sprays, gels, desiccants and hydrophobic powders applied to my dry-flies and have finally settled on what I consider to be the two best ways to keep my dry-flies floating. Thanks to the advice of Stuart Wardle to use Roman Moser Miracle Float, I use this gel when I want any dry-fly to float, including CdC. Close friends have other opinions but many find my method of treating a dry-fly works well for them. I follow the procedure below to rejuvenate a wet, fish-slimed, dry-fly.

1. Rinse the fly thoroughly in the river or lake to remove any fish slime and dirt.
2. Dry thoroughly by squeezing in a clean piece of absorbent kitchen paper. I don't like amadou or synthetic drying pads since after a time they become impregnated with floatant, dirt and fish slime and cease to be effective. A clever little trick is to twang the fly with a rubber band attached to your chest pack or vest to flick out any water.
3. Spread a drop of Miracle Float thinly between thumb and forefinger.
4. Rub the Miracle Float into your fly.

However, if I want a dark CdC fly to show up against a dark background I brush it with white hydrophobic fumed silica powder.

THE WASHING LINE METHOD ON RIVERS

The "washing line" method of presenting buzzers just below the lake surface on droppers, with a buoyant Booby or big dry-fly on the point and a floating fly-line, is a popular method on stillwaters, but I never see river anglers using it. On rivers the only multi-fly set-ups that I see are the Duo/Klink and Dink/New Zealand Dropper, where one or two nymphs are suspended under a dry-fly or a Czech-nymph/French-nymph/euro-nymph rig with two or three nymphs.

I must confess that it is only recently that I've been tempted to use the "washing line" presentation on rivers. It all started one early March day on an industrial Yorkshire river, when I was fishing for grayling with a pair of nymphs/shrimps on a Micro-nymph rig (0.55 mm diameter Micro-nymph line, plus a 6 ft/2 m tapered section from the middle of a tapered leader, 1 ft/0.3 m semi curly indicator and 6 ft/2 m of tippet with a short dropper 20 in/0.5 m from the point). Just after midday there was a decent hatch of large dark olives and the fish started to rise. Being unsure how long the hatch would last, I just removed the two nymphs and attached a size 18 CdC Shuttlecock on the leader point, something that I regularly do in such situations. This produced a few grayling but due to the brisk breeze and sunshine the LDO duns were immediately lifting off the water surface. I became aware that the fish were mainly rising to the nymphs just before they reached the surface. I had no unweighted nymphs so instead attached a size 16 spider pattern (a Japanese Kebari/reverse-hackled version of a Waterhen Bloa) on the dropper of the nymphing leader. Well over half of the subsequent takes came to the Kebari.

The big advantages of this set-up over fishing two spiders or unweighted nymphs were:

- With a dry-fly clearly visible just beyond the submerged spider I could clearly gauge any drag that was compromising my presentation.

- The visible dry-fly allowed me to determine the precise location of my submerged spider, making it far easier to see any takes to the subsurface fly. Sometimes the dry-fly gave the most obvious indication of a take as it skated across the surface.

- The dry-fly and greased leader ensured that the spider did not sink too far below the surface.

A PATERNOSTER RIG FOR NYMPHING ON RIVERS AND LAKES

Those of you who have used paternoster set-ups for coarse fishing or sea fishing will be asking yourselves, "How could such set-ups be relevant to flyfishing?" Well, here is my answer.

Firstly, let me describe the rig that I use. It consists of a leader with a dropper anything from 50 cm to 2 m from the point. My chosen fly is attached to the dropper (about 10 cm long) and at the point I attach a lead-free split-shot (anything from a number 10 to a swan shot depending on the river's

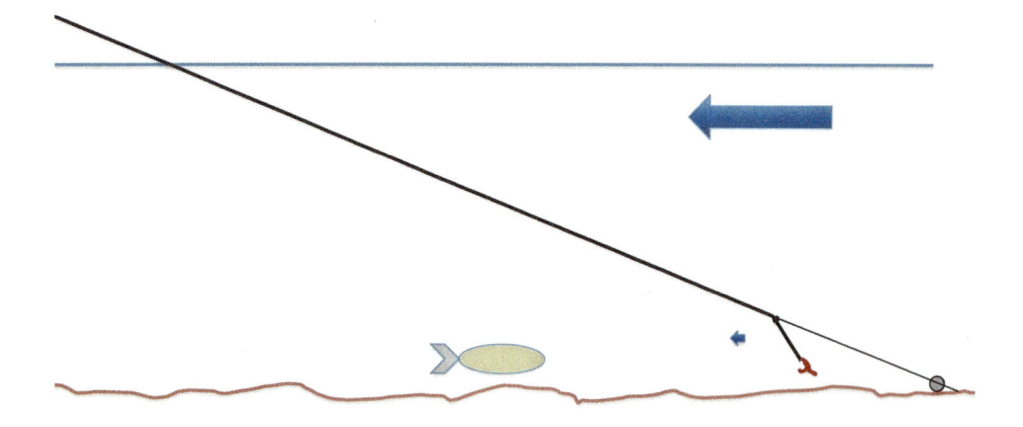

Diagram showing the key features of my method

A Wansford Lake grayling caught with the paternoster rig

depth and flow). The dropper and main tippet length of line is usually 0.15 to 0.13 mm copolymer and the point length is weaker, usually 0.13 to 0.10 mm (I'll explain the reason for this later).

I first used this set-up about fifteen years ago whilst fishing the fast inflow to my local small stillwater, Wansford Lake near Driffield. The stocked rainbows and resident grayling, plus an isolate wild brown trout, were clearly visible taking bloodworms close to the lake bed where the flow was quite slow. However, the surface flow was much faster which resulted in two problems. The first one was how to get a small bloodworm pattern (size 20) quickly through the fast surface water to the bottom 1 m below. The second was how to get my fly to drift at the pace of the lower water layers whilst the surface flow acting on my fly-line and leader was trying to drag my offering downstream at megaspeed. I didn't want to use a second, heavy fly on the point as there was a lot of weed in the area and a trailing fly might well have fouled on the weed resulting in a hooked fish being lost. The answer was to have a very long leader (5 m) so that the fly-line and much of the leader could be held off the fast surface water with a dropper 1 m from the point and a split shot on the point (nowadays I'd use a Euro-nymphing set-up). The shot not only took my small fly down to the bottom quickly but it dragged along the lakebed slowing down the drift to that of the subsurface flow. It took a bit of experimentation to get the weight of shot correct but when I did it resulted in a good bag of rainbows and a nice grayling of around 2 lb.

Since then I have used this set-up, mainly on rivers, in situations where I needed to get a single light fly down deep or when I've needed to control the drift rate. It has also proved useful in swims with a snaggy, rock-strewn bottom to help avoid the loss of too many flies (the weaker terminal length and the shot that relatively easily pulls off the end of the line means that I only normally lose a split-shot when I'm snagged up).

Another presentational advantage of this rig is that when I want, I can fish it like a drop shot rig on rivers or stillwaters, lifting and dropping to induce a take without fouling up a point fly with weed and debris from the river/lake bed. Furthermore, on rivers I can use a modification of the coarse fisher's stretpegging technique by fishing downstream, repeatedly lifting and lowering whilst feeding out line to allow my fly to progress downstream. The latter two techniques may be frowned upon by some traditionally minded flyfishers but they can be very effective, particularly when sight-fishing for grayling. I should add that a semi-curly bicolour indicator is very useful when using these two methods of presentation.

On stillwaters I have found this to be a useful way to effectively present a buzzer close to the bottom whilst using a bung and casting across or into a brisk breeze. The shot dragging the bottom slows down the drift, furthermore, the correct weight of shot occasionally catches on the bottom briefly stopping the drift and I have had a lot of takes just as the fly (or flies) started to move again. It would appear that this transition from static to moving is a real trigger for a fish to take, which is not surprising since bloodworms and buzzer pupae swim in short spurts with periods of rest when they either remain totally static or sink very slowly. Good presentation is generally all about showing the fish a fly that behaves naturally, sometimes with a slight exaggeration of natural movement.

Not everyone will approve of the tactics described here, but many may well have disapproved of the introduction of split cane rods with silk casting lines and reels when they first appeared on the scene – they must have been seen as giving an unfair advantage over the use of fixed lines. I must confess that I much prefer dry-fly fishing but there are many situations where an adaptive approach is the only way in which the capture of our target fish can be achieved. Some may well say, quite rightly, that catching fish is not the be-all-and-end-all of flyfishing, but for me solving presentational problems is a very important aspect of what I do whilst fishing and I derive great pleasure from finding a solution to a problem.

SIGHT-FISHING

The great appeal of dry-fly fishing for me is twofold; first, the chance to target rising fish, since this not only lets me know that they are actively feeding but it also tells me of their exact location; secondly, I can see the take instantly and can therefore judge exactly when to strike.

Blind-fishing/searching with subsurface flies can be rather hit-and-miss. Fish location is more challenging, requiring an intimate knowledge of the often, subtle signs that indicate a possible fish lie, a swirl of the current that signifies a submerged rock, a virtually indiscernible reduction in surface flow rate that tells us of a depression in the stream bed, plus the more obvious seams, fallen trees etc. Even when we've found these potential lies there may be no one at home. Then there is the problem of detecting a take. Some techniques are better than others for resolving this problem. The spider fisher can watch for a lift in the curve in his or her line, the French-/Euro-/Czech-nympher maintains a degree of tension in the line between rod tip and nymph(s) to aid bite detection when watching their indicator, whilst others may use a greased leader. In fast water any delay between the take and its indication will be very short and in some cases the force of the current may partially set the hook, preventing the fish from expelling the fly. However, in slow flows even a tiny amount of slack between the indicator (whether that be an actual indicator or just the line/leader) and the fly could mean that a take is not registered before the fly is rejected as inedible; in fact, the take may never register at all. A couple of days before writing this I watched a very big grayling take my shrimp and spit it out in an instant with no movement of my leader and no time to strike, even though I clearly saw the fly taken. To complicate matters even further, if the fish takes the fly and moves towards the angler any tension on the line will be reduced and no take indicated.

All this means that whilst blind-fishing with subsurface flies there is no doubt we get many takes that we never see. The only answer to this dilemma is to sight-fish whenever it is a feasible proposition. This is relatively easy when fishing in good light, at close range, on gin-clear, shallow chalk streams and spring-fed limestone rivers, but not so easy on most spate rivers. Nevertheless, even on the latter it is worth ensuring that you wear a pair of polaroid glasses for those few occasions when sight-fishing is feasible. In New Zealand sight-fishing is the norm on virtually all types of river thanks to the clear waters. So, let's look in more detail at the advantages and techniques of sight-fishing.

A major plus is the ability to precisely determine the location of one's target fish, with the possibility of selecting the biggest examples of the chosen species. On my local Driffield Beck, in autumn and winter I can distinguish the grayling from the unwanted trout by their forked tail, whilst in spring and early summer I can avoid the out of season grayling. Furthermore, I can cast specifically to the biggest grayling in a shoal and if a smaller fish tries to intercept my fly I can withdraw it, to ensure that hooking the smaller fish does not spook my intended target. On Driffield Beck grayling numbers are very low and precise location finding is vital (blind search-fishing is a

A big New Zealand brown trout, one of only four fish located in two miles of river

Returning a New Zealand brown trout

complete waste of time). Similarly, on many New Zealand rivers the trout are big but much less abundant than on the typical UK stream, so finding the fish is the first priority.

Precise location facilitates accurate casting, which reduces the risk of scaring the fish and increases the chance of a take. It is also helpful to land any subsurface fly a little to one side of the fish so that the take can be clearly seen as the fish moves to intercept the fly then returns to its lie. When casting, consideration needs to be given to refraction (the bending of light rays as they pass through the interface between water and air). A fish will appear to be further away and nearer to the surface than it really is (see diagram on page 24). Further thought needs to be given to the flow rate, nuances of current direction, the fish's depth and the sink-rate of the fly when deciding where and how far above the fish to cast. Fly sink-rate will be determined by the fly's density (weight and volume), surface area and shape, plus the diameter and material of the tippet, even whether the tippet is degreased. Dump-casts/parachute-casts aid rapid sinking of the fly.

Often fish will take a wet-fly on the drop (as it is sinking) or whilst it is dead-drifting (drifting naturally with the current); however, there are numerous times when the application of subtle movement to the fly may be required to induce a fish to take. I could recount many instances when a shoal of grayling has separated to allow my dead-drifted nymph or shrimp to pass them by, yet when I have given the same fly a gentle lift in front of their noses a fish has instantly taken it. Sometimes you will get a reaction as the fly is moved but no final commitment to take. It is then time to vary the angle or speed of the lift to see if that works. If a solid take is still not forthcoming a change of fly-pattern may be called for.

In order to judge when to apply subtle movements to the fly to induce a take, and so that takes can be clearly seen, it is an advantage to have highly visible flies. I tend to use quite bright orange or pink shrimp patterns or pale-coloured Utah Killer Bug variants with orange or pink butts and heads. Brightly coloured beads on Bead-head Nymphs are another option. I remember a day on the River Ure when I was acting as controller for a member of the Welsh Team – Kieron Jenkins – during an International Competition. Although Kieron could not see the grayling in this spate river he was using a white bead on his nymph to aid take detection. As soon as the bead disappeared from sight he'd strike and invariably there was a fish on.

Unfortunately, there are times when the fish will reject a bright fly. In the low water of October 2015, the Driffield Beck grayling were far more responsive to tiny Black Bead-head Nymphs and it was necessary to estimate the fly's location during the drift and watch the fish for any signs of a reaction. Takes were indicated in a variety of ways, some obvious, like a distinct movement to one side and a return to their original station, others much more subtle: such as a flare of the gills, an opening and closing of the mouth or a quiver of the pectoral fins. I strike/lift at any possible sign of a take. Timing the strike when takes are subtle is a bit hit and miss, with some fish just being pricked, but there is a decent conversion rate. It is much easier when you can actually see your fly disappear into the open mouth of your quarry, which brings me to angle of approach. It is often far easier to clearly see takes and apply subtle induced movements of the fly when fishing across or down and across the stream. However, on some waters the rule is "upstream nymphing only". Where this rule does not apply, ie when fishing downstream, particularly with trout, there is more risk of the fish being spooked by sight of the angler, since this is generally a close range tactic, so great stealth is required (camo' clothing, good use of cover, keeping a low profile and hyper-slow movements).

Finally, there is sight-fishing dry-flies to visible fish that are not rising. When there is no hatch many of my chalk stream fish caught on dry-flies are ones that I've located by sight but that are not actually rising. If I see a trout on the fin, above mid-water, I am pretty sure that it can be tempted to an appropriate surface offering (usually a size 14 Elk Hair Caddis or F Fly). If I only fished to risers my catch would be much depleted. I don't subscribe to

Halford's edict that one must only cast to a rising fish with a precise imitation of the fly species that it is taking. Not only do I catch a lot of non-risers in this way but I can also pinpoint the bigger fish.

So, if you've never tried sight-fishing, next time the water is clear enough to see the fish, put on the polaroid glasses (I prefer amber or yellow as they are effective even in low light) and give it a bash. It's great fun and very effective.

STREAMERS

I must confess to being a dry-fly addict, generally only turning to subsurface tactics as a last resort. I am also a light-line, delicate presentation addict so rarely fish with lines over three-weight; as a result, streamer-fishing is something that I very rarely do despite being well aware of its efficacy. I am certainly not against the fishing of streamers for trout and consider the slavish following of the Halfordian ethics of "upstream dry-fly only" to be outdated

Martin Smith fishing a streamer on a small South Yorkshire brook

SOME THOUGHTS ON TACTICS

and rather narrow-minded.

Flyfishers in the USA have been fishing streamers for trout as a standard practice for many years, as have reservoir flyfishers in the UK, but I've seen relatively few river flyfishers using these tactics. However, more and more river anglers are realising the potential of streamer fishing, particularly when targeting big predatory trout. Martin Smith, of Huddersfield, is one such person. In 2016, I joined him on a tiny headwater brook of a South Yorkshire stream and was amazed at the size of some of the trout that he extracted from its miniature pools with a small jig-hook streamer (Martin's Minnow). It is surprising how really small trout will take a streamer nearly as long as they are!

Pike, perch and zander are of course the obvious fish to target with

A Martin's Minnow

A Driffield Beck barbel that took a Martin's Minnow streamer

Pink salmon that took a Martin's Minnow

streamers, but there are other coarse fish that respond positively to a well-presented small fry fly-pattern. Recently I've been targeting chub and barbel using streamers, with encouraging success – catching chub up to 5 lb 4 oz and barbel up 10 lb 9 oz from my local Driffield Beck, plus wild brown trout to over 3 lb. Whilst targeting barbel, I also caught a large grayling, an 8 lb 2 oz sea trout and a male Pacific pink salmon!

My usual set-ups for fishing streamers are totally unconventional, as I generally only change from dry-fly to streamer fishing when I feel that it is appropriate. As a result, I just use my normal dry-fly gear. When streamer fishing on Driffield Beck, a chalk stream, I sight fish with a 10 ft four/five-weight rod, three-weight Micro Thin line and 12 ft of leader/tippet (7 ft butt from a 12 ft 6x tapered leader, tapering from 0.43 mm to 0.2 mm approx, plus 5 ft of 0.18 or 0.2 mm tippet, rather than the thinner tippet used for small dry-flies). On small streams I use a 7 ft or 8 ft one-weight rod with a one-weight, short head Micro Thin weight-forward line and 10 to 12 ft of leader/tippet.

Top: A pike streamer   Above: A decent sized fly-caught pike

When I'm fishing the turbulent pocket-water in the Austrian Alps I fish my streamers with a 14 ft 8 in Tenkara rod and a 0.285 mm diameter fluorocarbon line plus 3 ft of 0.15 mm tippet. Casting with such light set-ups requires an Oval- or Belgian-cast so that constant tension in the line is maintained and to avoid bead-heads hitting the rod. This works for me fishing at normal ranges on most rivers. The advantage of light lines and long leaders is that it is far easier to apply subtle movements to the fly by manipulating the rod rather than the retrieve. Barbel in particular seem to respond best to high-frequency twitching as the fly is slowly drawn along the riverbed.

Of course, on the very rare occasions that I've seriously fished for pike in the UK, or largemouth bass in Florida, I've used more conventional gear: for pike a nine- or ten-weight rod and for largemouth bass a seven-weight, with suitably tapered lines for casting bulky streamers and poppers. On waters holding big barbel a seven-weight set-up is far more appropriate than my rather inadequate light gear.

3

SOME THOUGHTS ON FLY DESIGN

FLY COLOUR

I have already stressed the importance of good presentation and said that I don't believe in magic flies, being of the opinion that in any given situation a range of similar flies will be equally effective. However, I do believe that our choice of fly should have the right triggers in order to convince the fish that it is food. These may be size, shape, colour, position on or in the water and movement, or a combination thereof.

I'll start by dealing with colour… Colour has been shown to be a powerful trigger for a number of innate (inbuilt) vertebrate responses. The Dutch ethologist, Niko Tinbergen, demonstrated that the red spot on an adult herring gull's beak stimulated the chicks' "pecking for food" response and observed their strengthened response when a model beak with a bigger area of red was used. Konrad Lorenz , Austrian zoologist, ethologist and ornithologist, noticed that male sticklebacks would attack anything red, even the image of a Post Office van seen through the glass of their fish tank, thinking it to be another male. Many fish appear to be "genetically wired" to respond to colours towards the red end of the spectrum. It is highly probable that the orange and red bellies of spawning brook trout and Arctic char, and red on the enlarged dorsal fins of male grayling, are triggers for courtship responses.

How does this relate to the colour of our flies? Most aquatic invertebrates

Male brook trout in autumn spawning colour

are well camouflaged, having cryptic colours of brown and olive, in order to avoid predators. The freshwater shrimp, *Gammarus pulex*, is typical, being a drab olive-brown. However, there is a parasite, an Acanthocephalan (spiny-headed worm, *Pomphorhynchus laevis*) larva that produces an orange cyst, making infected shrimps more attractive to the fish – the secondary host of the parasite. Also, during the breeding season shrimps develop an orange tinge caused by carotenoid pigments, which also colours the flesh of trout that binge on shrimps. I have had great success with Orange Spot Shrimps tied using fluorescent orange beads and with shrimps tied

Gammarus *infected with* Pomphorhynchus laevis *parasite*

using bright orange, spiky dubbing. Several of my best ever grayling, ranging from 2 lb 10 oz to just over 3 lb, fell to an Orange Shrimp.

Serratella (blue-winged olive) nymphs often have a distinctly rusty/orange tint and grayling in particular seem to be suckers for small orange Hare's Ear Nymphs. The late Dick Walker noted that the colour of blue-winged olive [BWO] duns was due to a blue exoskeleton covering an orange body. He used this to explain the success of the Orange Quill, a question that had confounded Skues. Walker believed that the fish were less sensitive to blue and therefore saw the fly with a more orange hue. Walker's BWO dun was tied with a mixture of blue and orange wool for the body. I must confess to being sceptical about the importance of colour in dry-flies, believing that the fish almost certainly see them as silhouettes, although there are those who would disagree with me. In the 1950s, Eric Horsfall Turner designed a tank to view dry-flies from below and noted that to the human eye colour was hardly discernible. At one time Walker's BWO was my standard pattern, but now I mostly use a size 16 IOBO Humpy as an emerging dun, or a CDC Gasparin Dun (my name for a fly that I believe to have been designed by Branko Gasparin of Slovenia).

Nevertheless, I'm keeping an open mind on the subject of colour and dry-flies, particularly those with submerged bodies, such as Klinkhåmers. Other flies in which orange has been very successfully incorporated include buzzer pupae where the wing buds have an orange tinge: I've found buzzers with fluorescent orange beads for the whole head/thorax to be very

Gasparin Dun

Pink Twinklehåmer *Pink Squirmy Worm*

effective. Then there is that old favourite of the spider fisherman, the Partridge and Orange, a fly which was never off my cast of two or three flies when I started flyfishing in the 1960s.

Pink has become a very popular colour in recent years. It was in the 1960s that Dick Walker mentioned pink with regard to shrimp patterns, which prompted me to experiment with patterns tied with a mix of hare's ear and bright magenta synthetic wool (similar to Antron). Why should pink be so effective against trout and grayling, when it seems to be absent in the aquatic environment? If you ever catch an American brook trout take a close-look at the tiny spots on its flanks – they are bright pink. They must be important to have evolved and been retained (probably species recognition). There is no doubting the effectiveness of pink, particularly for grayling. I use bugs and shrimps from subtle to garish pink to great effect. Mike Weaver in his book on wild trout mentions the success of a pink may-fly pattern. I often use a pink glister Twinklehåmer (on which I caught loads of grayling on a 2007 trip to the Rajamaa Fish Camp, Sweden). I have found pink Squirmy Worms to be very successful with brown trout, rainbow trout, cutthroat trout, brook trout, and grayling.

Red has long been recognised for its appeal, witness the popularity of the Red Tag, fished wet or dry. I have found bloodworm patterns in various

Size 20 Bloodworm (red bead, red holographic tinsel and red flexi floss)

guises to be excellent not only for stillwater trout, but also for trout and grayling in rivers. When tying them my main concern is to achieve the bright, translucent effect of the natural. With the use of flexi floss, Dick Walker's Red Rubber Band fly has evolved into the Apps Bloodworm. Red holographic tinsel ribbed with red wire or red flexi floss on a grub hook also works well. I add a black tungsten bead at the head if I want to achieve depth. For those with zero tying skills, small red glass beads threaded and Super Glued onto a grub hook make a first-class imitation.

Another favourite pattern of mine is a Copper Head Nymph with a red wire abdomen and hare's ear thorax.

Yellow? Not a colour I often use, but when the yellow mays are emerging on free-stone rivers I wouldn't be without Oliver Edwards' Yellowhammer. I also tie some of my sedge pupae in bright amber/yellow, whilst some of my Peeping Caddis have yellow bodies. Maybe I should experiment more with this colour since annatto maggots were great catchers of coarse fish when I was a

Yellow Catgut Caddis Larva/Pupa (wetted)

Serricostoma caddis larva removed from its case

kid, and sweetcorn is the choice bait of many who trot for grayling in the winter (when it catches lots of out of season trout as well): not a natural bait, but devastatingly effective.

Green has its day. *Rhyacophila* larvae, some cased caddis larvae, some caddis pupae and damsel nymphs are often quite bright green. I like to exaggerate the brightness to increase their appeal. Some people like a green tag (egg sac) on their dry sedges, particularly on a Grannom.

Catgut Rhyacophila *Larva/Pupa*

Purple... Oliver Kite introduced purple thread into his classic Imperial to imitate olive duns. Jesper Larsson, the chief guide at Rajamaa, uses to great effect, a monstrous purple Klinkhåmer, the Purple Ugly. The Snipe and Purple is a classic wet-

Rhyacophila *larva*

fly (probably imitating the iron blue), which I rarely had off my cast in the 1960s. I also have a purple Zonker, given to me in Alaska by a guy fishing for rainbows: he described it as "the best rainbow fly ever!" I've only used it once, since I rarely fish with lures, but it caught well then. Friends do very well for grayling with a Purple Nasty, a bug tied with a purple glister collar, CdC hackle and hare's ear dubbing body.

Blue is a colour I've neglected. Fish are reputed to be less sensitive to this end of the spectrum and yet blue light, being shorter wavelength than red and higher energy, penetrates much deeper into the water. Davy Wotton has mentioned the effectiveness of tiny blue Buzzers in *Fly Fishing and Fly Tying* magazine, and the Teal Blue and Silver was once a respected fly for both trout and sea-trout.

Black... A complete lack of colour! I'm finding myself using black flies more and more. I believe that their success is largely due to the strong silhouette that black flies make against lighter backgrounds, particularly the sky. It has long been recognised that black flies are very effective for nocturnal sea-trout, but many experiences have convinced me of their value in spate conditions. In such low light we want something the fish can see. Many years ago, my automatic response to highly coloured water was to increase the fly size and use bright pink Shrimps or Gold-head Nymphs with bright orange bodies. I'd catch a few fish, but never many. Then, in 2009, during a spate on Pickering Beck I'd fished large bright flies for an hour with no success. In desperation I changed to my favourite nymph, a Black-bead Pheasant Tail in size 20. I immediately started catching both trout and grayling, ending with over 30 fish in a couple of hours. My second such experience was also on Pickering Beck, during a spate in May 2010. I nearly returned home on seeing the water, but a single riser showed me that fish were feeding. It transpired that the gale, which was blowing branches off the trees, was also dislodging thousands of aphids. A size 26 black CDC IOBO Humpy accounted for twenty trout despite water the colour of milk chocolate. Nowadays, my first response when seeing heavily coloured water is to fish with a black nymph or black streamer.

There's no doubt that there are times when colour, or lack of it, can be a very important factor in deciding whether a fish will accept our offerings.

FLY SIZE

The second trigger that I'd like to consider is size. Often, when the fish are not preoccupied with specific food items, the exact size and choice of fly is relatively unimportant. Trout are generally opportunistic feeders. One only has to look at the stomach contents of the average trout to see this. I once caught a brown trout with a large bullhead still protruding from its mouth. On looking at its gut contents I found several small black beetles, a couple of *Baetis* nymphs, a few large dark olive duns and a hawthorn fly. However, there are times when the fish may be totally preoccupied with one food item. This most often occurs when there is an abundance of tiny invertebrates or small fish available. At such times it can be essential to use flies which are as near as practical the same size as the food source, the fish being unable to associate anything bigger with food. Fish have very small brains and therefore seem incapable of processing too much information at once. As a result, they can develop a very simplified "food image" when certain foods are abundant. This innate adaptation makes them more energy-efficient feeders. This one-track mindedness is also why fish that are mad on feed are surprisingly difficult to scare and why spawning fish seem completely oblivious to any other stimuli. Even I, with a far superior brain, find multi-tasking difficult!

So when might we expect this preoccupied, size-dependent feeding to occur? Any time of the year... Much depends on where you fish.

On my local small stillwaters we get hatches of tiny micro-midges in every month. The adults look like specks of soot drifting on the surface, whilst the pupae are like commas from a piece of newsprint. A realistic imitation would be tied on a size 36 hook (if you could get one). When I see the typical head and shoulders rise-form of midge feeders I usually start with size 24s tied to 6x tippet in the hope that the fish aren't too preoccupied, and I drop to size 30s tied to 7x or 8x tippet if I get too many refusals. Going too light is a problem, since I hate protracted playing of sizeable fish with the attendant risk of lactic acid build up in their muscles and subsequent death, if not thoroughly nursed back from exhaustion. A size 24 fly on 6x tippet is a compromise between adequate presentation and protracted landing time (7x or 8x would give far better presentation). I regularly use a loop knot (Rapala Knot) for attaching the fly to tippet if I feel that the fly is being held too rigidly for good presentation to be achieved. This permits much freer movement than a fixed knot with relatively stiff tippet. Having thoroughly evaluated the practice I am convinced that it improves my presentation of such small flies. Jesper Larsson, who guides at Rajamaa Fish Camp in northern Sweden, showed me the knot and swears by it for reducing micro-drag when fishing dry-flies in turbulent flows. It certainly worked well for me using larger flies when I visited Rajamaa in August 2007.

Size 30 Wire Buzzer Pupa and the real thing

Patterns need to be kept simple for tiny flies. For adult midges I use either a CDC IOBO Humpy, or a Minimalistic Micro Midge (just a tuft of CdC tied onto the hook shank). For the pupae I use either a size 24 Black Beadhead Stripped Quill Buzzer tied with a 1.5 mm tungsten bead or a size 26 to 30 Buzzer Pupa tied with 0.09 mm wire coated with UV resin. Micro-midges are also a significant food source on most rivers. With global warming and the decline in upwinged flies they are becoming more so every year. Grayling, in particular, can become besotted with them to the exclusion of all else. Here again a simple size 24 to 30 dry-fly or Midge Pupa may be all they will look at, provided it is well presented (micro-drag free).

In late July and early August thrips or thunder bugs can blow onto the waters near to cereal crops. Once again, a size 26 to 30 thin-bodied IOBO Humpy or Minimalistic Micro Midge is the answer. A few years back, on the Yorkshire Rye, during a hatch of small dark olives, I was having a frustrating time as the trout were inspecting, but refusing, my size 18 Parachute Olive. It was not until I noticed the thunder bugs on the water and changed to a size 26 IOBO Humpy that I was rewarded with slow, confident, rises from both trout and grayling.

Caenis *dun (photo Stuart Crofts)*

On some rivers and stillwaters dawn and dusk throughout the summer can see massive hatches of tiny *Caenis* (the "fisherman's curse"). Early in the hatch the fish mainly take the nymphs since the duns seem to explode out of the shuck, never resting on the surface. However, the duns soon transpose into spinners, which mate, egg lay and die within half an hour. It is then that the surface can be plastered with tens of thousands of prostrate corpses. You might stand a chance with a size 22 Spinner, but as mentioned earlier, a dragged size 20 Griffiths Gnat seems to provide an added trigger, stimulating the fish to select the artificial from the plethora of prostrate spent natural spinners.

In late spring and autumn aphids are often at their peak of availability. Strong winds in late April and early May dislodge these prolific insects, whilst leaf fall in autumn often deposits vast numbers on the water. At such times I call on a size 24 to 30 IOBO Humpy or Minimalistic Micro Midge tied with natural grey CDC (colour seems to be unimportant). In June 2019, Don Stazicker came to my local Pickering Beck to do an article for *Trout and Salmon* magazine. Despite a reasonable

Aphids on alder leaf

number of emerging big mayflies (*Ephemera danica*) the trout were preoccupied with a glut of aphids. Don and I ended up fishing with size 30 aphid imitations in order to achieve any significant success.

The iron blue is another small fly, which, although sadly in decline, is a favourite of trout and grayling. I don't know why nearly all the commercially produced iron blue imitations are size 16, because the natural flies I see on the water are more like a size 20. Towards the end of the 2007 trout season I had an invite to fish Foston Beck, a lovely little northern chalk stream. There was a good hatch of assorted olives and the fish were rising like metronomes. I tied on a size 16 Paraloop Olive: no response. A size 16 CDC Gasparin Dun: no response. A size 16 IOBO Humpy: still no response! Frustration was setting in – the hatch might be short-lived and I was missing out... I was getting close to using unparliamentary language when I noticed, mixed in with the olives, a few iron blues. A change to a size 20 imitation resolved the problem. The result: sixteen fine trout landed in a little over an hour, after which the hatch ceased.

Iron blue dun, male

When is a big fly necessary to trigger a feeding response? On my local Yorkshire Derwent I am restricted to the dry-fly during June, July and August: when there is no hatch and the fish are loath to surface feed, a big fly like a Daddy or large sedge will often prompt a rise. I don't for a moment credit the trout with the conscious thought: "That's big enough to be worth the effort..."; it's all too easy to anthropomorphise, giving the fish powers of reasoning. I believe that the size and the relatively splashy landing of such big flies provide strong enough triggers to induce the reflex feeding response. Many years ago,

I had some great fish from the Tay at Aberfeldy, in the middle of the day when nothing seemed to be moving, by fishing a size 10 F Fly to simulate the isolated large stoneflies I had seen. The response of the fish was explosive.

In August, in Swedish Lapland, despite virtually no rising fish, the grayling would take a large Klinkhåmer or sedge with gusto: the dry-fly well out-fished nymphs and bugs.

Dinocras cephalotes *stonefly*

So, next time you're failing to get takes to your fly, consider size – it may be a significant factor. In particular, don't be scared to try really small flies. The fish can see them: if you use Orvis 4641 Big Eye hooks or Gamakatsu C12-BM midge hooks that have oversized eyes they are not hard to tie on. If you keep the patterns simple and use a lens they're not difficult to tie and they are surprisingly good hookers and holders of fish.

EXTENDED BODIES

More and more often I find myself modifying standard fly-patterns in an attempt to make them more effective. There are several key criteria that I feel are essential for a fly to be well designed:

- It must have the correct trigger features required to elicit either a feeding or an aggression response from the target species of fish. Ideally, I believe, these features should be exaggerated to more readily prompt the desired response (supernormal stimuli).

SOME THOUGHTS ON FLY DESIGN

- It should fish at the right depth on, in or below the water surface.
- It should be as easy as possible to cast, not over heavy, air resistant or unbalanced.
- The design/construction should not prevent it from being easily engulfed by the chosen quarry.
- It ought to be durable. I expect my flies to survive at least 30 trout before they show signs of serious wear and tear.
- It ought to be simple to tie.

One design feature that can significantly enhance many dry-fly patterns (particularly the larger ones) is the use of flexible extended bodies. A major advantage is that with a smaller, short shank, a lighter hook can be used. This facilitates more delicate presentation, aids floatability and in addition reduces the number of lost fish due to leverage against the long shank hooks used traditionally for Mayflies and Daddies.

Let's consider the various types of extended body that I have used and the advantages they confer.

Feather Bodies
(wonder-wing style)

At one time I used these for many of my Mayfly and Spinner patterns. Their advantages are that they are very simple to make, look great, are translucent like the real thing, are naturally buoyant and are incredibly light. Their lightness means that, on a calm day, I can effectively cast big Mayflies with my one-weight rod. So why do I rarely use them now? My main reason is their lack of durability. Also, the larger Mayflies tied this way, have a large surface area to mass ratio making them quite air resistant and difficult to cast into a wind. Furthermore, they are quite stiff which might occasionally prevent them from being easily engulfed by the fish.

Foam Bodies

I use sealed cell foam sheeting and cylinders for my Grasshoppers/Crickets, Ants and some of my Daddies and Mayflies. It is very buoyant, so great for flies used as indicators when fishing the Duo/New Zealand Dropper method. It is also soft, fairly flexible and quite durable.

Furled Polypropylene/Antron Yarn Bodies

At one time I used these for most of my Daddies and Mayflies. Although less buoyant than foam they float quite well. They are simple to tie, soft, flexible and very durable. At the 2010 Newark Fly Fair I saw some nice midges tied with extended bodies made from furled CdC fibres.

Micro-Chenille Bodies

These have become my favourites for my Daddies, Mayflies, Hawthorn Flies and Black Gnats. Until I saw a Swedish fly-tyer demonstrating at the 2009 Newark Fly Fair I did not know how to tie tails onto flexible bodies. Now

I do. Chenille bodies are even simpler to use than furled yarn. Synthetic micro-chenille is naturally hydrophobic (water-hating) so floats very well and doesn't get waterlogged. It is very light, soft, flexible and durable. One day, in late May, I had 30 brown trout from Pickering Beck, on the same micro-chenille Mayfly and a few days later I had 70 brown trout, from the upper Yorkshire Derwent, on the same chenille bodied Daddy, with no significant signs of wear.

Silicone Sealant Bodies

Stuart Crofts showed me some of his dry-flies tied with extended bodies made from silicone bathroom sealant and dubbing, using a needle to form the body. They were amazing. He even had size 24 Midges tied with extended bodies. I've not got around to trying the method he described to me yet but I must – silicone sealant is naturally buoyant, hydrophobic, strong and flexible.

Let's now consider how to make some extended bodies.

FEATHER BODIES

Take a suitably sized and coloured cock hackle (other types of hackle can be used). Fold back the lower fibres (as shown overleaf) and smear sparingly with flexible glue, silicone sealant or nail varnish. Stroke the fibres together whilst the glue is still wet and hold in place till it sets. Clip out the feather tip, leaving a couple of fibres each side as tails (if tails are wanted). Tie in a small ball of dubbing at the bend of a short shank hook: this will prevent the top of the feather body from puckering up too much when it is tied in. Tie the body onto the ball of dubbing. After this the rest of the fly can be tied.

1. Pull back feather fibres, coat with flexible glue, silicone sealant or nail varnish.
2. Trim out feather tip, leaving tail fibres. Varnish and hold back fibres until set.
3. Tie body onto a ball of dubbing.

FOAM BODIES

Segmented bodies, with or without a tail, can be tied using 1 or 2 mm thick sealed cell foam cut into a strip with a slight waist and a small notch cut at the waist (the sample shown is the right size for a Mayfly). Mount a suitably sized needle into the vice. Lay down a short (3 to 4 mm) bed of thread towards the tip of the needle. If a tail is required tie this onto the needle tip (as shown). Take the foam strip inserting the small V-shaped slot over the end of the needle and fold the strip either side of the needle (for small flies the small notch is not needed, just push the needle tip through the slight waist in the middle of the foam strip). Wrap 5 or 6 turns of thread around the folded foam, 1 or 2 mm from the end, to create the end segment. I then do a half-hitch for security. Fold back the foam and wind the thread up the needle (as shown). Fold the foam back alongside of the needle and then wind the thread around the foam to create the next segment. Repeat this procedure until the body is long enough and secure the thread with a whip finish or a series of

SOME THOUGHTS ON FLY DESIGN

half-hitches. Pull the body off the needle, trim the ends (as shown) and it is ready to be tied to the hook.

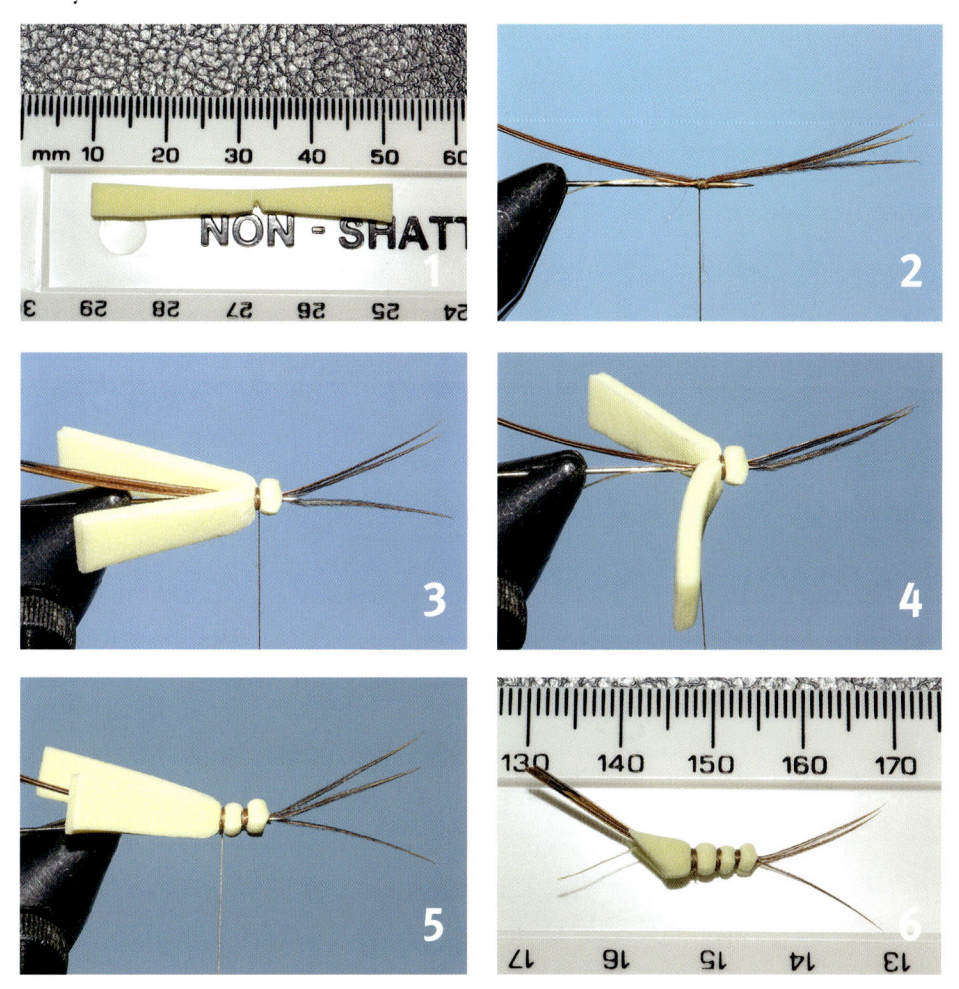

1. Cut foam strip to shape.
2. Tie tails onto a bed of thread on a needle.
3. Mount foam on needle and tie first segment.
4. Advance thread on needle.
5. Tie next segment(s).
6. Whip finish. Remove body from needle and trim end before tying to hook.

FURLED YARN BODIES

Take a short length of polypropylene yarn (about 6 cm long) and under tension twist repeatedly. Then whilst holding both ends release the tension and the yarn should automatically twist into a furled "rope". Tie this onto the hook. If you want to add a tail, clamp the furled body into your vice with only the last 2 mm projecting. This holds the flexible body tip rigidly enough to tie on a tail (as shown, making sure you whip finish, trim and add a small drop of Super Glue to the whipping).

1. Tie body to hook and mount body in vice (as shown). Then wind thread 1 mm from end of the body.
2. Tie on tails and whip finish.
3. Trim tails and thread and apply small drop of Super Glue.

You can now finish the fly with hackles, wings etc.

MICRO-CHENILLE BODIES

These are the simplest bodies to tie. Just singe the end of the chenille with a flame to seal it. If you wish, tie on tails (as shown for tying tails to furled bodies) and tie the body onto the hook.

My favourite hooks for extended body dry-flies are:

- Tiemco 206 BL, Grip 14723 BL (wide gape, short shank, barbless, fine wire).

- Tiemco 2488 (wide gape, short shank, micro-barb, medium fine wire, strong).

- Tiemco 2499 SP BL (wide gape, short shank, barbless, medium wire, very strong).

Sizes 12 or 14 are perfect for Daddies and Mayflies and size 18 or 20 for Black Gnats.

If you haven't tried extended bodies do so, they are very effective and surprisingly simple to tie.

CDC

CdC, Cul de Canard, duck's bum fluff, call it what you will, these feathers from around the preen gland of ducks (and geese) have magical properties. Their structure, which has a massive surface area of fine barbs, and possibly the natural preen oil, makes them naturally hydrophobic (water repellent). They are also highly mobile giving life to the fly. Also, being very light means that any aerial parts of the fly made of this material do not weigh down and submerge the supporting fibres in contact with the water surface.

Records show that CdC has been used in the Jura region of Switzerland for over one hundred years. Highly popular with the French and East European flyfishermen I have met, it is seen in increasing numbers of boxes belonging to UK flyfishers. Some folks still shun the use of CdC. It may be that they suffer from some of the misconceptions which prevented me from taking CdC seriously until relatively recently:

1. The delicate looking fibres are too fragile. *Wrong!* I expect to catch at least 30 trout or grayling on a single fly. Well-tied CdC flies are remarkably durable.
2. Once a CdC dry-fly is wet it is useless and must be replaced and left to dry naturally. *Wrong!* I heard this misconception repeated at the 2006 Fly Fair by a very well-respected supplier of fly-tying materials and have read it more recently in articles and books. For a number of years this old wives' tale limited my use of CdC flies to occasions when all else failed. Drowned CdC flies, particularly those coated with hydrophilic (water attracting) fish slime, are easily restored to service by the following: *Thoroughly wash* in the river to remove any slime; *dry carefully* by squeezing between pieces of kitchen paper (or Amadou); *give a thorough rub* and then blow on the fly to *fluff up the fibres* (barbs). In addition, you might wish to *apply an ultra-thin coating of CdC Oil, Roman Moser Miracle Float or brush over with hydrophobic Fumed Silica powder* to prolong the flies' water repellence. I expect to catch twenty or more fish without having to change my fly. The time spent washing and drying is not wasted; it is spent watching the river (or lake) for fish activity, lining up the next victim!
3. CdC is difficult to tie with. *Wrong!* Using a few basic tying techniques it is one of the most versatile, easy to use materials available to the fly-tyer. My favourite CdC patterns are all very simple. I see no virtue in tying complex patterns when simple ones work.
4. CdC is very expensive. *Wrong*! Good quality CdC is not cheap, but neither are high quality genetic capes. If you use it as I suggest later (see p 150, point 6), every last fibre of each feather will be incorporated into flies. If you know somebody who goes duck shooting your CdC could be free, or maybe be just cost you the price of a pint of beer.

My real conversion to CdC started in April 2002. Due to the Foot and Mouth epidemic, I was unable to fish the rivers and so had to fish on my local stillwater. Finding that the rainbows were intent on eating tiny emerging midges I tied up some size 20 Shuttlecock Buzzers. The fish loved them. This was my first significant use of CdC. Then a friend discovered the IOBO Humpy on the Internet. This lethal fly was devised by Pennsylvanian angler Jack Tucker in 1996. IOBO stands for It Oughta Be Outlawed. In sizes 20 to 30 you'll not find a better fly for fish fixated on tiny insects in the surface film, whether they are aphids, midges, thrips, or smuts. They fool even those hyper-fussy fish on the glass-smooth glides that will look at a size 22 Paradun or Klinkhåmer but reject them. In sizes 14 to 20 the IOBO effectively imitates emerging olives, black gnats and egg-laying stoneflies. It has proved to be a real get-out-of-jail fly for me and my friends. The other great thing about the IOBO is that it must be one of the easiest of all dry-flies to tie.

My conversion to CdC was further facilitated in 2004 when I read about a CdC Olive devised by the renowned Slovenian fly-tyer, Branko Gasparin. I call it the "Gasparin Dun". This simple, no hackle pattern is now one of my mainstays when the duns of olive and pale wateries are about. The tall CdC wing acts as a parachute, gently lowering the fly to the water. This plus the widely spread moose hair tails ensure that the fly lands and sits upright on the water virtually every cast. With its thin body it provides trigger points that make it one of the most effective dun imitations I have ever used. Much to my amazement, despite the lack of a supporting hackle, this fly will ride high on even quite turbulent water.

My conversion was completed by the success I had in 2005 and 2006 with two other simple CdC flies: Marjan Fratnick's excellent F Fly, a first-class imitation of sedges and stoneflies, and the dry CdC Spider, which is suggestive of a host of insects trapped in the surface film.

On two of my fishing holidays I fished nearly exclusively with CdC dry-flies. The first a September trip to Slovenia. Steve Donohue and I targeted the grayling of several famous rivers including the Sava Bohinjka, the Unica, the Tolminka and the Soča. Nymphing proved relatively ineffective compared with the dry-fly. Around 9.30 in the morning, as the sun started to burn off the morning mist, stoneflies became active and a size 16 IOBO Humpy with two widely spread wings proved to be a perfect fluttering stonefly imitation. Steve opted for a size 16 CdC Spider that was equally well-accepted. This main rise only lasted for about an hour, after which isolated stoneflies and olives stimulated only intermittent interest from the grayling. Nevertheless, in the gin-clear water it was easy to spot the fish. By casting to the occasional riser, or covering visible fish with a size 16 F Fly, CdC Spider, or Gasparin Dun, fish were steadily caught throughout the day. At dusk there was sometimes a brief rise to midges and pale wateries. Then a size 18 or 20 Gasparin Dun, F Fly, CdC Spider, or IOBO Humpy did the trick. Over 80 per cent of my six-days' tally of 236 grayling and trout fell to CdCs.

The second was a June trip to Poland's River San, where virtually all of my 90-plus trout (up to 4 lb 8 oz) and 47 grayling (to just over 2 lb) fell to CdC flies, mainly F Flies, and a few to CdC Emergers and IOBO Humpies, all in sizes 18 to 20.

Since then I've been experimenting with CdC Klinkhåmers, substituting CdC for both the wing and hackle. They have proved very effective for both grayling and trout in the UK and cutthroat trout in Yellowstone Park, Wyoming.

There are several things I've learned whilst experimenting with and fishing with CdC:

1. It helps if all the materials to be used are either naturally buoyant and water repellent, or they have been pre-treated with a good floatant such as Watershed, or wax. The only exception to this is when I want part of the fly to sink eg the abdomen of Klinkhåmers and Shuttlecocks, or the shucks of Emergers.
2. Do not apply conventional floatants to CdC as they will clog up the

The four types of CdC

barbs/fibres. However, I have used CdC Oil since the spring of 2009, and find it very good if applied sparingly, but now prefer Roman Moser Miracle Float applied very thinly or hydrophobic fumed silica powder brushed into the fly.

3. Tie in the CdC with a couple more thread turns than normal as CdC is quite slippery.
4. If possible use light wire hooks – there is a vast variety available these days.
5. Choose the right type of CdC feather:

   Type 1. Short, broad, straight-ended feathers with thin stems are great for IOBO Humpies, Shuttlecocks and F Fly wings.

   Type 2. Longer, thinner straight-tipped feathers with long barbs that virtually all reach the tip, and thin stems, are good for all the above plus roped to make CdC bodies and for loop wings.

Type 3. Long feathers with more rounded tips and shorter barbs that are of relatively even length and have thicker stems are fine for Mayfly wings. When roped they can be used to make straggly, semi-palmered bodies and when their barbs are trapped on a thread loop they can be used to make CdC hackles for the CdC Spider, or Klinkhåmers. They are not much use for other purposes.

Type 4. CdC puffs, very short feathers with no stem, are fine for the wings of small Emergers, Shipman's Buzzers and small Shuttlecock Buzzers (and Mayfly Nymph gills where their movement and texture are the important features).

6. When using long feathers save any discarded butt sections and use the barbs either for CdC dubbing, or trap in a bulldog clip, insert into a split thread and use for CdC hackles. Thus all the CdC is used, none is wasted.

7. If using a bulldog clip, as a substitute for a Mark Petitjean CdC tool, stick thin strips of 1 mm sealed cell foam along the leading edges of the clip to ensure a good grip on the CdC fibres. This is particularly important whilst cutting away the main stem of the feathers and whilst inserting the barbs into the split thread.

8. My favoured threads for splitting are Uni Trico 17/0 (a very fine, white Dyneema type thread which can be coloured with permanent felt tips) and Uni thread 8/0 (which comes in an assortment of colours). To split them easily use a magnifier, stretch the thread over your index finger to spread the fibres and insert a <u>sharp</u> needle (*carefully!*). I then insert my index finger into the split to keep it open whilst inserting the CdC barbs from the bulldog clip.

Of course, the use of CdC is not confined to dry-flies. Its highly mobile fibres/barbs are ideal for nymph legs and tails, Sedge Pupae legs, wet spider hackles and Mayfly Nymph gills to mention a few.

If, like me, you've put off the use of CdC because of misconceived

SOME THOUGHTS ON FLY DESIGN

notions regarding problems with its use, give it a try. You'll be amazed at its effectiveness and versatility. I assure you that you too will become a convert.

"ANCHOR-BODIED" FLIES

I'm sure that we are all well aware of the often-deleterious effects of drag when it comes to tempting trout (and particularly grayling) to take our dry-flies, but some of you may be less aware of the micro-drag which we are generally unable to see, but which the fish can all too readily detect. I was firmly reminded of this on a fishing trip to New Zealand's Southland in 2011. In the heat of the day the brownies were cruising the slack water under the overhanging willows, sipping down tiny willow grubs that were falling out of the red/brown galls covering every leaf. Repeatedly I had fish cruise up to my floating, yellow foam

Willow grub galls

Willow grub

Foam Willow Grub

New Zealand trout

imitation only to turn away at the last moment despite what appeared to be a good drift. However, in most cases, persistence paid off. Repeated casting to the target would eventually result in a confident take. I am absolutely convinced that the rejections were due to micro-drag. In one case I spent over 30 minutes on one fish that was working a back eddy where drag avoidance was virtually impossible. Eventually I achieved my aim by trimming down the foam Willow Grub until it almost sank. This anchored my size 18 fly into the surface and delayed micro-drag just long enough for the fish to be fooled.

So how can we avoid/reduce micro-drag? All the slack-line casts in the world will not reduce micro-drag, which is caused by the influence of aberrant currents pulling/pushing the tippet close to the fly. One partial answer is the use of very fine, flexible tippet material (this is why I use copolymer rather than the stiffer fluorocarbon). Flexible tippet is particularly important when fishing tiny flies that lack the inertia to resist even the smallest of forces exerted by the tippet. It is also very important when using well-greased flies that sit on the surface and are held free of the surface tension by hydrophobic (water-repelling) forces; this renders them vulnerable to even the slightest deviant movements of the tippet. The use of a loop knot (Rapala Knot or Perfection Loop) to join the fly to the tippet can significantly reduce the linkage between the tippet and fly and thus reduce or delay the onset of micro-drag.

In addition to these there is a further way to limit micro-drag. More and more I find myself fishing with dry-flies that sit low in the surface film and that are anchored in place, albeit weakly, by hydrophilic (water-loving) hydrogen bonds between water molecules and their submerged bodies. So how can our dry-flies be designed or treated so that they will anchor well into the surface? We not only need a significant part of the fly to sink below the surface but these parts of the fly must be wetted so that they will bind to the surrounding water molecules. Any tying materials used for these parts of our fly must be dense enough to sink and must not be water-repellent (hydrophobic). Floatant should be applied to wings/hackles and sinkant or

SOME THOUGHTS ON FLY DESIGN

saliva (which is hydrophilic) should be applied to the subsurface body of the fly. Let's consider a few of my favourite semi-submerged patterns:

Shuttlecocks

Over the last few seasons small Shuttlecock Emergers have become some of my most used and most effective flies. In a range of sizes they imitate emerging Chironomid midges, emerging Ephemerids (upwings/mayflies) and a range of half-drowned terrestrial insects. When tying them it is critical to balance the weight of the submerged body with the amount of CdC wing needed to effectively support it. To facilitate instant sinking of the body in small sizes (18 and smaller) I either use fairly heavy wire grub hooks and stripped peacock herl coated with Super Glue (or more recently UV resin) or alternatively fine wire straight-shanked hooks with a body of very fine dubbing and a rib of fine copper wire.

Klinkhåmers

Hans Van Klinken's original Klinkhåmer was, I believe, intended to imitate an emerging caddis but it has morphed in its various versions into a highly effective general emerger pattern. Part of its success, I am sure, is that the substantial body anchors well into the surface. In larger sizes I like to tie mine with a body of Ice Dub or Glister ribbed with extra-fine copper wire, which not only sinks well, but also does not hold too much water and so makes casting more pleasant and less splashy when large Klinks are used.

Spent Spinners

Baetis spinners (large dark olive, iron blue dun and many others) lay their eggs underwater and never break back through the surface film when spent, whilst blue-winged olive spinners and mayfly spinners, which lay their eggs by dipping to the surface, sink into the surface film when spent. I tie my olive Spinners with CdC wings tied in a V shape, bodies of unwaxed thread and tails of white or grey organza fibres. I apply CdC oil or Roman Moser Miracle Float to the wings and tails only and saliva to the body.

Viewed from under water

Hawthorn Flies/ Black Gnats

The naturals tend to sink into the surface film as they struggle to escape its grasp. As a result, the only part of these flies to which I add floatant is the white poly-yarn wing.

SOME THOUGHTS ON FLY DESIGN

Elk Hair Caddis/F Flies

I cock up the wings with horizontal thread wraps under the wing and small head (made from the butts of the elk hair or CdC). Here again I apply floatant to the wing only. If I want extra anchorage I tie them on grub hooks to aid body-sinkage, as does the use of a body of UV resin-coated stripped peacock herl. (If I want to twitch, dance or skate my sedges I tie these patterns conventionally on straight-shanked hooks and with more buoyant bodies coated with floatant.)

F Fly tied on a grub hook

Foam Beetles

Get the balance between the amount of foam and the hook weight right and these will subside into the surface film like the real thing. However, this makes them very hard to see unless you add a bright poly-yarn sighter – to which I add floatant.

Suspender Buzzers

Like the Foam Beetles, these too need the correct balance between hook weight and amount of foam. I use foam cylinders to provide the buoyancy. If you tie the cylinders a bit too big you can then trim them down till the fly only just floats.

Stuart Crofts' Ant

Stuart designed this fly specifically, as he put it, to "rivet" the fly into the surface film to help resist drag. This variant on the F Fly, in sizes 20 to 16, makes a good imitation of a number of terrestrials that tend to sink into the surface film, including smuts, ants and ichneumonid flies. A coating of UV resin applied to the abdomen and waist not only looks great but also facilitates rapid sinking of the body.

What about submerged tippets? I must confess that I never apply sinkant to my dry-fly tippet since I want a clean lift off when I cast and when striking. Also, since I use CdC flies for most of my dry-fly fishing, I do not want a sunken tippet drowning my flies (if at all possible I do not want to have to false cast to dry my flies since this is one sure fire way to spook fish). However, sunken tippet next to the fly is possibly another way of providing some anchorage. Many anglers subscribe to the view that sunken tippet is important so that the fish are not frightened by the sight of the tippet. I am not convinced about this since, as mentioned earlier, when fishing tiny flies (sub-24s), I often use a highly visible loop knot to reduce the influence of the relatively stiff tippet on my offering. Furthermore, whilst fishing size 18 Willow Grubs in New Zealand I often resorted to 3x (8 lb) tippet in order to stand a chance of landing my quarry, and I found that the fish took confidently when I got the presentation right. A potential disadvantage of a submerged tippet which I've observed is that sometimes a fish noses the tippet whilst attempting to take the fly often resulting in either the fly being pushed away from the taking fish or the fish bolting in panic.

Another answer to the problem of micro-drag that was suggested to me by both Stuart Crofts and Stuart Wardle, after I'd had a frustrating time trying to avoid drag on the pocket-water of the upper Tees (before I got into short-line Tenkara fishing which resolves most, but not all, drag problems), is to fish a Klink and Dink/Duo/New Zealand Dropper set up with a weighted nymph suspended a short distance below the dry-fly, so that the nymph acts as a drogue. I have at times used this to good effect but find I miss quite a few takes to the dry-fly, particularly when grayling fishing. This could well be due to the tensioned tippet between the dry-fly and nymph preventing the fish from taking the dry-fly properly.

There are of course many situations where drag can be an asset, for example when fishing with sedges at night or when mayflies are emerging and skittering across the river surface, but much of the time drag, even virtually imperceptible micro-drag, is the kiss of death to success when dry-fly fishing. It can never be totally eliminated but it can be managed with a bit of thought and good fly design. As with many things in life it is an accumulation of little things that can lead to success or failure. If you want to catch more fish forget about the top of the range rod and reel and concentrate your efforts on the small, apparently insignificant things like micro-drag.

NB: Unfortunately there are some fisheries where emergers and semi-submerged dry-flies are banned, making life more difficult for the angler but reducing pressure on the fish (a mixed blessing!).

Tying a Stuart Crofts' Ant

Hook *Grub size 20 to 16*
Thread *Black 8/0*
Body *Fat abdomen and thorax of thread separated by a waist of red holographic tinsel and all coated with Bug Bond Lite*

Wing and head *Three natural CdC feather tips*

Tying an F Fly Variant

Hook *Grub size 24 to 10*
Thread *Brown 8/0*
Body *Stripped peacock herl coated with thin UV resin (or Super Glue)*

Wing and head *Three natural CdC feather tips*
Thorax (optional) *Either CdC fibres in split thread or dubbed hare's ear/mask fibres*

VISIBILITY

How is your eyesight? Fortunately, mine is excellent (at least when wearing glasses) despite over 70 years of use. I can still see to tie size 30 dry-flies onto 8x tippet and in the right conditions can still see such small flies when fished at sensible ranges. However, there are many times when even relatively large dry-flies are hard to see and there is even more of a problem when sight-fishing with nymphs and bugs.

I hate not being able to see my fly! I know it is possible to estimate fairly well where the fly is and to react to a rise in the correct general area or to a subsurface movement of the nymphing fish (a flare of the gills, sudden movement to the side or sharp movement of the pectoral fins). However, if the fly can't be seen you are unable to assess whether there is any drag (even a trace of micro-drag can put fish off) and you don't know exactly when to subtly lift your nymph/bug to induce a take from that fussy trout or grayling that doesn't want it dead-drifted.

If it comes to a choice between using a natural-coloured imitation or fishing a visible pattern I'll nearly always go for high visibility. I know there are people who believe that the brash, bright posts/sighters on dry-flies will spook a lot of fish but in my experience this is just not the case. In fact, there is evidence that in some instances vividly coloured variants actually attract the attention of feeding fish, a phenomenon known as "oddity selection", which I mention in the section on *Gammarus* and the added appeal of shrimps that are parasitised by the spiny headed worm, *Pomphorhyncus laevis*, which gives them a bright orange spot. My philosophy in flyfishing is "suck it and see" and I'll continue to tie garish, highly visible flies till the fish tell me that they don't like them.

So, when is visibility a potential problem and how do I try to resolve it when it is?

Seeing micro dry-flies can be very difficult in all but the best light even at close range yet I often find myself using size 24 to 30 midge/aphid patterns for fussy fish that are preoccupied with tiny "invisible" on or in the surface film. In such situations the upward pointing wing (in dark CdC) of a small Shuttlecock or IOBO Humpy will show up surprisingly clearly in most lights. With dark background reflections or in very broken water fluorescent pink or orange CdC has proved to be effective, as has coating a natural pale grey CdC wing with white hydrophobic fumed silica powder. When fishing Micro-suspender Buzzers I usually find a white foam-cylinder head is easy to see, but again bright pink or orange make a good alternative. I often use parachute Daddies or Klinkhåmers with a bright orange foam-cylinder post as an indicator when fishing the Duo method.

Size 30 Orange CdC Midge

Hi-vis Iron Blue Dun

Seeing even quite large dry-flies on boiling, foam-flecked pocket-water can be a nightmare. I love such water since it is perfect for one of my favourite methods of fishing – Tenkara. In such places I find there is nothing to beat a bright, fluorescent pink poly-yarn dyed CdC or sealed-cell foam post/wing.

Dusk on a warm summer's evening is a great time to be fishing with either a dry sedge/caddis or a spent olive spinner pattern. The spinners, in particular, can be almost impossible to see, since they must be fished sitting right down in the surface film. I have two solutions to this problem. If the background is dark I'll fish with an Elk Hair Caddis tied with bleached elk (virtually white) or a Paraloop Pheasant Tail Spinner tied with a white hackle (the half-dome hackle shows up well whilst allowing the body to sit in the surface film). If the water surface is bright, particularly when fishing into the evening glow, I'll fish an F Fly tied with natural dark CdC or a CdC-winged Spent Spinner (the wings of both show up clearly as silhouettes against the light). It is also worth considering tying some flies with black poly-yarn sight posts to be used against bright background reflections. My friend Glen Pointon has devised spinner

Glen Pointon's luminous flies
(coated with watchmaker's luminous powder and exposed to UV light to activate)

and sedge patterns with foam posts, coated with luminous dust (mixed with varnish), that glow brightly after exposure to light from a UV torch. He has had great success with these when fishing after dark in summer and very kindly sent me some. I too have had success with them.

Other patterns that sit low in the surface film are the Super Pupa, an excellent imitation of a sedge pupa swimming in the surface film, and Foam Beetles. I tie both with a bright pink yarn sighter.

Hi-vis Super Pupa

SPIDERS

When I was first introduced to flyfishing in the late 1960s I always had at least one spider pattern on my three-fly cast. Typically, in early season (April) I'd have a weighted shrimp on the point with a Snipe and Purple Spider on the first dropper and a Partridge and Orange Spider on the top dropper. As things warmed up I'd change the point fly to a Sawyer Pheasant Tail Nymph. Then, once the fish started rising well, I'd change to a Partridge and Orange on the point, Snipe and Purple on the first dropper and a dry Greenwell's Glory on the top dropper. These combinations worked well on the upper reaches of the Yorkshire Rye where most of my flyfishing was done. Nowadays I rarely fish with spiders, much preferring the visual aspects of dry-fly fishing when possible and fishing heavy nymphs, shrimps and bugs during the winter for grayling, however I am coming to realise that spiders still have a useful place in my repertoire of techniques.

Since 2010 and my discovery of Tenkara and the fantastic presentation that is possible with these long, fixed-line rods I have done some fishing with

The author Tenkara fishing a Kebari in the pocket marked with the arrow

the reverse-hackled Sakasa Kebari flies that many Japanese Tenkara fishers use. These are very similar to our traditional North Country spiders but with the hackle fibres facing forwards over the hook eye so that, when pulsed, more movement/life can be imparted into the fly. In Tenkara fishing the casting line is very light (generally brightly coloured 0.285 mm diameter fluorocarbon) and is about the same length as the rod (typically about 3 to 4 m) with about 1 m of fine tippet. With rod held high only the fly and the tippet are allowed to touch the water, which helps to avoid drag from vagaries of the river current acting on the line. Takes are indicated either by seeing

Woodcock and Orange Sakasa Kebari

the fish flash at the fly or by watching the end of the coloured fluorocarbon line for any unusual movement. Although I prefer to fish with dry-flies on my Tenkara gear, subsurface Kebaris are very effective.

Now I know that the traditional way to fish spiders is as a team of two or three with a long rod, casting them up and across the river and tracking them down to give a drag-free drift – possibly followed by allowing them to swing under control when they are downstream of the angler, takes being indicated by a lift of the slight sag in the line – but I have found fishing a spider plus a dry-fly emerger on a washing line set-up is a great way to fish. It all started on a windy, sunny March day when the large dark olives were lifting off rapidly and the grayling were rising to nymphs in and just below the surface film on an industrial Yorkshire river. I had been having limited success with my size 18 Shuttlecock and since I had no unweighted nymphs with me I attached a Waterhen Bloa Kebari Spider on a short dropper about 18 inches above my Shuttlecock Emerger. The result was a significant improvement in my catch rate with most fish coming to the spider. This rig gave me several advantages:

- With a well-greased leader and dropper my spider stayed just below the surface film.
- Having the dry-fly on the point allowed me to see when drag was setting in.
- The dry-fly helped me to pinpoint the location of my spider making it easier for me to see any takes and if I did not see the swirl where my spider was I certainly saw my dry-fly skate away when the spider was taken.

Waterhen Bloa Kebari Spider

A big Driffield Beck grayling taken on a Silver Bead-head Partridge and Hare's Ear Spider

Most of the waters that I fish are quite small streams and many of the clubs only allow use of a single fly; as a result, I often fish upstream using a relatively short rod and a single spider using a greased leader to indicate any takes. If the water is very broken or the light is poor, making a greased leader difficult to see I fish using a greased semi-curly tricolour monofilament indicator plus about 3 ft of tippet.

I am not a traditionalist so I often use Bead-head Spiders in order to fish a single fly at depth, particularly for winter grayling. A Silver Bead-head Partridge and Hare's Ear Spider has accounted for several 3 lb plus

Bead-head Waterhen Bloa Spider (1.5 mm black tungsten bead)

Partridge and Hare's Ear Spiders

grayling from my local Driffield Beck and numerous smaller grayling from a variety of waters. It has also accounted for plenty of trout.

Some of the best grayling fishing of the year is in the autumn and early winter so maybe that's the time to get the spiders into action!

From top: Chironomid midge adult; Chironomid pupae, mm scale; Chironomid larva

4

SOME THOUGHTS ON ENTOMOLOGY

WINTER AND MIDGES

There are over 400 species of Chironomid (non-biting) midge or buzzer in the UK. Adults of some species may be 13 mm long, but most are between 1 and 5 mm. Colours vary from black, grey, brown, yellow, orange, red and green (sometimes a mix of more than one colour, for example red and black). The larvae are present in virtually every freshwater river and lake in the world, even those that are quite badly polluted, and they are particularly abundant in waters with a silted bed. The larvae feed on organic detritus, algae, fungi and bacteria. The large numbers of bloodworms found in many lakebeds have been linked to the abundance of methane-eating bacteria (which feed on methane gas released from the breakdown of organic matter in the lake sediments). Below sewage outfalls in rivers are prime sites for high populations of Chironomid larvae and I know of one grayling hot spot on a Derbyshire river that is just below the town's outfall.

It always amazes me how few flyfishers fish with tiny midge imitations, particularly in winter when midges are generally the only flies to hatch. There is not a single day in the year that some midges do not hatch on our lakes and rivers. Every stillwater flyfisher knows that one of the major food items of stillwater trout is the Chironomid midge pupa or buzzer, but they generally use flies that are huge compared to the natural insect that they are supposed to be imitating. Most river flyfishers seem however to be unaware of the importance of midges in the diet of their quarry. Furthermore, even fewer folks consider fishing with tiny dry midge patterns in the winter, yet I've had some amazing dry-fly sessions on cold, miserable winter days.

I was reminded how good winter dry-fly fishing can be a few days before writing this. It was a raw, damp, late November day with a maximum air temperature of 6°C. A couple of weeks earlier friends and I had experienced amazing grayling fishing during leaf-fall, fishing with size 24 to 30 CdC dry flies. However, on this late November day I said to my two companions that I thought our chance of any dry-fly fishing was virtually nil and that we'd be nymphing. Arriving at 10.30am we saw a grey, cold, uninviting looking river, but it wasn't long before I noticed a single riser in a smooth, shallow glide. As we cautiously waded into the river we saw a few other grayling rising to "invisibles". A close inspection showed there to be a few tiny adult midges on the water. We needed no further invitation. We each attached size 26 to 30 CdC midge imitations (IOBO Humpy, Shuttlecock and Minimalistic Micro Midge) to light tippet and so started one of the best dry-fly fishing sessions we've had for a long while. The fish were not easy to tempt, often demanding repeated presentations of the fly until that perfect, drag-free drift was achieved, but we caught fish steadily all day long. I also found that I had increased success with a size 30 fly compared with a size 26 or 24. There are times that fly size can be critical to consistent success! Stuart Crofts, who lives further up the river, tells me that there is virtually not a single day in winter that grayling cannot be seen rising to midges on the River Don in Penistone, where he lives.

The same is true of my local small stillwater, Wansford Lake, near Driffield. In fact, the best midge hatches occur during the winter and the best of these during the 2017/18 winter were around dawn and dusk on the coldest, frostiest days, particularly on the dull days when we had snow flurries. At such times I had great fun fishing a size 26 to 30 CdC Minimalistic Micro

January grayling caught on a size 30 CdC dry Midge

Midge to the rising rainbows. With a bit of thought it is obvious that cold conditions should provide good surface activity when midges are hatching as the river or lake water is a usually a relatively warm 4° C or more whilst the air may well be below freezing: being cold-blooded the adult midges need warmth in order to have enough energy to fly off, but without sun and with very low air temperatures these adults become "locked" on the water surface, easy prey for the fish. Several times I've found an area of the lake where the wind has concentrated accumulations of these tiny adults and there have been "wolf packs" of fish mopping them up.

Of course, there are days when the grayling or rainbows are focusing on the midge pupae whilst they are resting just below the surface film, pre-emergence. This often occurs on slightly warmer days when the adults are not lingering on the water surface. At such times a tiny Shuttlecock Emerger or Suspender Buzzer (with a foam head), fished in the surface film is my choice of fly.

*Stomach contents from a rainbow trout caught in winter
– all three main life stages of the insect present*

On other days it is the ascending pupae that are of interest to most of the fish and a tiny Wire Buzzer or Bead-head Buzzer suspended from a small dry-fly, greased leader or greased semi-curly indicator is my choice of approach. In calm conditions I prefer a greased leader, since many takes come on the drop as the fly slowly sinks and with a greased leader it is easy to see any change in the rate at which the fly is sinking, a sure indication of a take!

We mustn't forget the larval stage, of which the most commonly imitated variety is the bloodworm. The red colour is caused by haemoglobin which helps the larvae extract oxygen from the relatively anaerobic silt within which they spend much of their time. However, in well-oxygenated waters, particularly rivers, the larvae of most species are not red, but olive, yellow, pale brown or green. I must confess that the only realistic larval imitation that I use is a red one, tied on a size 20 short shank hook with a 1.5 mm red or black tungsten bead head and body of red holographic tinsel, plus tail of half-thickness red flexi floss or the thin red pole elastic used by coarse anglers. This I fish on the drop using a greased leader, suspended deep down under a small dry-fly, or suspended from a greased semi-curly monofilament indicator.

As I've said earlier, good presentation is one of the biggest challenges when fishing with tiny flies. Bloodworms and midge pupae swim incredibly slowly, often drifting inertly with any flow of the water (even so-called stillwaters have currents caused by the wind and surface flows may be very different from subsurface flows). Whilst freshly stocked rainbows will tolerate the most unnatural of presentations, (such as a pulled Bloodworm, or one

Top: Rainbow caught on a size 24 Buzzer Pupa
Above: Grayling caught on a size 20 Bloodworm

drifting in an arc), educated wild fish and long-term resident fish will usually studiously ignore any badly presented fly. Buzzers and bloodworms fished on the drop must sink vertically, not in an arc, so they must be cast with a dump cast and not on a tight, straight line. Fine tippet must be used not just so that it will fit through the tiny eyes of the size 20 to 30 hooks needed to accurately imitate most Chironomid species, but also so that they are supple enough to facilitate natural movement of the fly. Long tippets will ensure that there is some slack near to the fly to further facilitate natural presentations.

As for rods and lines; long, soft-actioned rods teamed up with light lines

*Size 24 CdC IOBO Humpy (Tiemco 2488)
and size 30 Minimalistic Micro Midge (Gamakatsu C12-BM) (mm scale)*

are essential to protect light tippets whilst playing good-sized fish. I love my 10 ft two-weight rod teamed up with a one-weight Micro Thin line or a zero-weight line. For super-delicate fishing, even for big fish, my choice is a 10 ft 6 in zero-weight rod with either a zero-weight line or Micro Nymph line. With both set-ups I use a 12 to 14 ft leader made up of a 7 ft long tapered section (tapering from 0.43 mm to 0.20 mm diameter cut from the butt of a 12 ft 6x tapered copolymer leader). At the end of the tapered section I have a small perfection loop to which I can attach a semi-curly mono bicolour indicator (loop to loop) then 5 to 7 ft of 0.10 mm or 0.09 mm tippet, or just the tippet.

It is virtually impossible to buy tiny midge patterns so the only viable options are to tie your own or find someone who will tie them for you. It is also very difficult to buy strong midge hooks in suitably small sizes in the UK. My two favourite tiny hooks (at the time of writing) are Tiemco 2488s (at the time of writing only available down to size 26) and Gamakatsu CM12-BM (available from size 26 to 30); both are short shank, wide gape hooks. The Gamakatsu hooks have the advantage of having extra big eyes. In the UK it is possible to buy Orvis Big Eye dry-fly hooks and the identical Daiichi 1110

SOME THOUGHTS ON ENTOMOLOGY

Size 28 Wire and UV Resin Buzzer Pupa (0.09 mm wire and Tiemco 2488 hook)

hooks, which are the same shank length as size 24 Tiemco 2488s but with quite a narrow gape. Other hooks available in the UK that I have found to be reliable are Daiichi 1120 (heavy wire Grub hook down to size 22) and 1130 (fine wire Grub hook down to size 24). Whatever the fly-pattern it needs to be simple when tied on tiny hooks.

LARGE DARK OLIVES

In the winter of 2018/19 I had some amazing dry-fly fishing for grayling on the Yorkshire rivers and for rainbows on my local small stillwater (Wansford Lake). In all cases the fish rose to microscopically small midges and I had to drop down to size 30 CdC flies to consistently tempt the fish. This necessitated the use of soft-actioned light-line rods (10 ft two-weight and 10 ft 6 in zero-weight) teamed up with light lines (one-weight Micro Thin, Micro-Nymph or zero-weight) and very light tippet (0.09 mm diameter). However, things changed as we got into March and April of 2019; large dark olive (LDO) time.

On my local rivers LDOs start to emerge from any time in late February and hatches steadily increase up to the end of April. The best days are usually dull and often quite cool. The best ever hatch of LDOs that I've seen on my local Yorkshire Derwent was on a dull day in mid-April with the air temperature 4°C and flurries of sleet and then snow. On bright, warm, windy days any flies that hatch are soon warmed up and away before the grayling or trout have much of a chance of catching them.

There is no point going to the river early if you want dry-fly action as LDOs

Large dark olive (female dun)

Baetis spinner

Shuttlecocks

Stuart Crofts' Spent Baetis *Spinner*

rarely emerge before midday. I aim to arrive about 11am and head for the pool-heads below any shallow riffles, since these flies generally emerge from relatively shallow, well-oxygenated, gravelly/rocky runs, particularly where there is a good growth of *Ranunculus*. In February and March hatches may be very short-lived, whilst later on they may last well into the afternoon.

Before the hatch starts I often fish a small (size 18) Bead-head Hare's Ear or Stripped Quill Nymph in the riffles and pool heads, but once I see my first riser on goes a size 18 Shuttlecock Emerger or a size 18 CdC IOBO Humpy. I use the same light-line gear that I've used when fishing midges but with the larger flies I increase the tippet size to 0.10 mm or 0.13 mm diameter. If it is windy and warm and the LDOs are lifting off rapidly I've done quite well fishing a Shuttlecock on the point and a size 16 Waterhen Bloa Spider on a dropper about 2 ft from the point, with most fish taking the spider. The Shuttlecock helps me to see when drag sets in, helps me judge exactly where my spider is so I can easily see takes, and if I don't see the take to the spider the Shuttlecock acts as an indicator. After the hatch has ceased sometimes the fish will continue to rise to midges as these tiny morsels are about most days of the year. When the hatch has stopped and if there are no more rises then Stuart Crofts has a useful tactic and that is to fish a sunken *Baetis* Spinner pattern tied with a 1.5 mm tungsten bead. The logic of this tactic is that *Baetis* spinners (most of the olives) crawl under the water to lay their eggs and the spent spinners never break back through the surface film.

BIBIONID FLIES

Hawthorn fly (male) and its imitation

Hook Size 14 short shank, eg, Tiemco 206BL or similar
Thread Black 8/0
Extended body Black Andre Brun polychenille
Hackle Black cock trimmed underneath

Wing White poly-yarn
Head and thorax cover 2 mm thick black sealed cell foam
Legs Knotted peacock herl

Late April is the start of "terrestrial time". The 25th of April is St Mark's Day, the time when the hawthorn fly (*Bibio marci*) traditionally appears. Some years there is a glut of these relatively big, gangly-legged Bibionids: at such times, on sunny, breezy days, clouds of them may be seen taking shelter behind bankside tree cover. They are not particularly strong fliers and many get blown onto the river surface where they get trapped into the surface film, easy prey for the trout. Any suitably sized black fly will work but for aesthetic reasons I like a reasonably imitative pattern. I apply floatant to the wing only, so that the body subsides into the surface, like the real thing, and also this anchors the fly into the surface thus resisting micro-drag. If a dead-drift fails to tempt the fish the application of tiny twitches to simulate a struggling fly can be very effective. Close range fishing with a long rod and light line is a big advantage when applying subtle movements; if the fish aren't too big a long Tenkara rod with a level line of 8 lb fluorocarbon plus tippet is ideal. Alternatively, a 10 ft or longer light-line rod with a Micro Nymph line and 12 ft plus leader would be my choice.

Black gnat (female) and its imitation

Hook	*Size 18*	**Hackle**	*Black cock trimmed underneath*
Thread	*Black 8/0*		
Body	*Fine black poly dubbing*	**Wing**	*White poly-yarn*

SOME THOUGHTS ON ENTOMOLOGY

May is for me the black gnat (*Bibio johannis*) month. This is a smaller Bibionid, best imitated on a size 18 hook (18 short-shank if tying a pattern with an extended body). As with the hawthorn fly, clouds may be seen sheltering behind trees and hedges on windy, sunny days and they frequently get blown onto the river surface. Some of these casualties will be mating pairs and a Double Badger is a good, simple pattern to imitate these.

If you see large numbers of either of these flies on the water you might well expect that any rising fish are taking them but beware as there are times when the trout for some inexplicable reason are focused on taking something completely different. I remember two days whilst guiding on Driffield Beck when the river was covered with both hawthorn flies and black gnats that were being totally ignored. Instead the fish were vigorously taking *Agapetus* sedge pupae (see the next section on the importance of *Agapetus* pupae). I have known other times when tiny midges or tiny beetles have been the preferred choice of the fish; so keep an open mind and use your eyes.

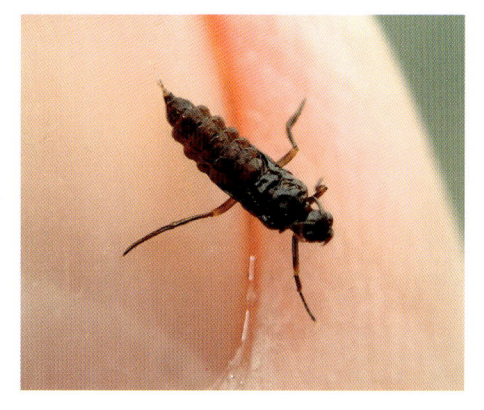

AGAPETUS PUPAE

Agapetus *larva (mm scale)*

Agapetus *pupa*

Agapetus *adult*

Stuart Crofts' Agapetus *Pupa*

As an enthusiastic fisher of tiny flies, I had long been aware of 5 mm long micro-caddis of the genus *Agapetus*, but it was not until a few years ago that Stuart Crofts (probably the UK's top expert on caddis flies) enlightened me to the fact that the vulnerable stage in their life-cycle is the pupa as it swims to the bankside vegetation where it will transpose into the adult. Stuart has devised the perfect fly to imitate these tiny (5 mm long) pupae as they swim in the surface film towards the riverbank.

The three most common UK representatives of this genus, *Agapetus fuscipes*, *Agapetus ochripes* and *Agapetus delicatulus* are all very similar. Their larvae make 3 to 5 mm long, igloo-like cases from tiny particles of gravel. On my local East Yorkshire chalk stream there are so many chalk gravel cases to be seen in summer that the *Ranunculus* beds often look as though they are covered with dandruff and 3-minute kick samples contain up to 8000 of the cased larvae. The tiny moth-like adults are rarely seen on the water, but during the summer may be found scuttling about in the bankside vegetation. The pupae are what we anglers need to be aware of, if our rivers contain them in any significant numbers. To check their abundance look for 5 mm pebble igloos covering the rocks in the river.

Emergence of *Agapetus fuscipes* in East Yorkshire starts in early May during the daytime and continues till late summer with two peaks of activity around June and August. The main sign that the fish are focused on emerging pupae

Big fish on an Agapetus *Pupa*

is when you see fish rising quite aggressively to what I call "invisibles» (rises to black gnats, midges and spent spinners are usually quite leisurely). A further sign of such fish activity is that your midge/aphid/spinner pattern is being completely ignored despite accurate casting and drag-free presentation – although you might get an occasional response to a small dry-fly just as it starts to drag. A final sign is that fish preoccupied with *Agapetus* pupae are virtually impossible to spook, even by careless casting.

Stuart's *Agapetus* Pupa is tied on a size 20 Partridge SLD or similar hook, with fine orangy-brown dubbing (I usually use brown), two CdC kicking legs each side (or one each side of microflash) and two mini white poly-yarn posts. The body is wetted with saliva so that it sinks and a touch of floatant is applied to the tips of the posts to hold the fly horizontally in the surface film. (Stu is a genius at fly design: simple and effective!) Fish it up and across, dead-drifted, with frequent small pulls to make it swim (they swim remarkably fast for their size). Expect vigorous takes, so take care when striking since you'll probably be using 6x tippet. A long, softish, two- or three-weight rod is ideal for this, fishing to protect the fine tippet and aid subtle manipulations (thick, heavy lines tend to damp down the fine movements required to simulate natural movement). Tenkara is an alternative if the fish aren't too big. A further way to enhance the presentation is to tie your *Agapetus* imitation into a loop knot (Rapala Knot or Perfection Loop) to give it more freedom to move.

Don't think it is just small fish that will focus on *Agapetus* pupae: the biggest fish in the river will come out for this feast. So, check if you've got them on your river and tie up some imitations.

HEPTAGENEIDS

March is the month during which many flyfishers think about that classic Heptageneid, the March brown, *Rhithrogena germanica*. This species has suffered a decline over recent years (as have many other upwinged species) but there are encouraging signs of recovery on some rivers. Its strongholds are big, rocky, spate rivers including many of the Scottish rivers, the Cumbrian Eden and the Welsh Usk and Wye. Hatches tend to occur around midday between March and May and in my limited experience the fish rise quite vigorously to them. This big brown fly is often confused with the very similar large brook dun, *Ecdyonurus torrentis,* which emerges a little later in the spring (mainly during May in my local North Yorkshire streams). The key distinguishing feature of the March brown is a distinct dark mark on the centre of an otherwise pale femur. A popular fly amongst friends who regularly encounter hatches of this fly is a size 12 or 10 Jingler.

I often come across the large brook dun, *E. torrentis*, during May. Here again, a size 12 or 10 Jingler takes some beating as an imitation.

Large brook dun

Other very similar "big brown jobs" include the large green dun, *Ecdyonurus insignis*, which has a very localised distribution, and the autumn dun, *E. dispar*, which emerges later in the year.

The spinners of these species all have very similar rusty brown bodies. A size 12 Pheasant Tail Spinner pattern is a suitable pattern when the spinners return to the river to egg-lay, when they will be seen descending to the river to dip their abdomens in the surface.

One fly that can be easily confused with the above species and is not a Heptageneid, is the turkey brown, *Paraleptophlebia submarginata*, which is common on many of the North Yorkshire Moors streams that I fish (and I've also seen good numbers on the upper Yorkshire Don). It emerges from late April through to July and the dun looks like a small, dark March brown/large brook dun. The turkey brown is less significant to the flyfisher as emergence from the nymphal exoskeleton often takes place partially or entirely out of the water on emergent rocks or vegetation. Nevertheless, I've seen fish taking them and I fish with a size 14 March Brown imitation.

Large brook spinner

Turkey brown dun

Also in May I expect to see good hatches of olive uprights, *Rhithrogena semicolorata*, on many of the stony rivers that I fish. This is a smaller fly than its larger cousins and its wings lack their brown mottling. Emergence can

LONG RODS—LIGHT LINES

Olive upright dun (minus a tail)

Yellow may dun

Heptageneid nymphs

take place throughout the day and a size 14 olive imitation is a good choice when it does so. The dark mark on the femur, and broad head, clearly distinguishes it from the similar but slightly smaller large dark olive, *Baetis rhodani*.

In June and July, the yellow may dun, *Heptagenia sulphurea*, emerges on many stony rivers. Many writers have questioned whether trout find them palatable, but on my Yorkshire streams there is no doubting that the fish feed on them. It may be the fact that hatches often occur as trickles on many rivers that make some anglers doubt their importance as trout food. The duns are a very distinct bright yellow and a size 12 Oliver Edwards' Yellowhammer (a yellow Klinkhåmer) works for me when they are emerging.

What about the nymphs? They are "stone clingers" with sturdy legs and flattened, triangular, streamlined bodies. It is possible to tie realistic imitations, as did Oliver Edwards, but I just fish a Black Bead-head Hare's Ear

Nymph with a large bead at the head to give the triangular shape and I sometimes add rubber legs.

A deep knowledge of entomology is not essential for success in flyfishing, but it can help at times and is a fascinating activity in its own right. My good friend Stuart Crofts now spends more time studying aquatic invertebrates, particularly caddis flies, than he does fishing!

Please note that hatch times can vary significantly depending on the latitude and altitude of the river.

APHIDS

Trout and grayling can become totally preoccupied with any super-abundant tiny food source to the exclusion of all else. These include *Caenis* spinners, Chironomid midges (particularly adults and pupae), thrips (thunderbugs), *Agapetus* sedge pupae and particularly aphids. At such times it is usually essential to fish a suitably small fly-pattern with an appropriate presentation.

There are at least 600 species of aphid in the UK and most are quite species specific with regard to the plants on which they feed. All species are very small, generally from 2 to 5 mm long. Colours range through black, brown, green, yellow and orange. Winter is usually spent as cold-resistant eggs, often on the buds of the host plant. There are two adult life stages: in spring the eggs hatch to produce mainly wingless females that reproduce by parthenogenesis (asexual, with no need to mate) and population numbers can explode early in the year. The offspring, which are all clones of the parent, are live-born (no eggs). Aphids feed by piercing with their hollow mouthparts the host plant's food-carrying tubes (phloem) in the stems or leaves. The pressure within the phloem is such that sugary sap is forced into the aphid's stomach and not all of this is absorbed, some is released as honey dew from the aphid's anus. Ants often feed on this sugary waste and cars parked under trees with heavy aphid populations get covered with sticky droplets. In late summer and autumn (into November) a winged adult stage appears with both male and female forms. These mate, in order to achieve genetic variation, and then lay eggs that survive the cold of winter.

Sycamore trees, common along the banks of many of our rivers, are a great source of aphids, hosting at least eight species and it is primarily in areas of river where sycamores are abundant that I search for aphid-feeders. Alder trees, common along the banks of many rivers also support good aphid populations and seven species have been identified feeding on the common European alder. The best times to find aphids on the water are windy days from mid-May and throughout the summer, but the main glut as far as the fish are concerned is often at leaf-fall and when the winged adults are in flight during October and November. Let me recount some classic examples of top-notch dry-fly fishing for aphid-feeders…

The first was a day in mid-May a few years ago, on Pickering Beck in North Yorkshire. The river was swollen and badly coloured after heavy overnight rain and it was blowing a gale. Why I chose to go fishing on such a wild day I'll never know. On seeing the river, I nearly returned home but fortunately I saw a fish rise in a tiny bankside eddy and decided to look above the mill weir where the water is slow and deep. The river surface was covered with debris, branches and masses of fresh, young leaves that had been ripped off the overhanging alder trees by the gale. Trout were rising steadily despite the heavily coloured water and a close inspection of some of the leaves showed them to be covered with tiny green aphids. Dodging the falling branches and with great difficulty because of the gusting wind, I cast my size 24 CdC IOBO Humpy to the rising fish and in a relatively short time I'd landed around twenty feisty little wild brown trout. It was a great fishing session – all thanks to the gale and the aphids.

The second instance was a couple of days in mid-November, 2018, on an industrial Yorkshire river that has a good number of sycamore trees along its banks. The weather was remarkably mild and leaf fall was well underway. On arrival, fish were rising steadily and in big numbers along a glide next to where we'd parked the car. The river surface was covered with leaves and there were a huge number of aphids drifting down in the surface film. Stuart Crofts, Steve Donohue and I had an absolute bonanza with the grayling. We fished with a range of size 24 to 30 dry-flies. Hook size proved to be a critical factor. Having started with a rather overdressed short-shank size 24 CdC IOBO Humpy I found that I was getting far fewer takes than I had anticipated and was missing quite a few of the takes that I did get. A change to a size 30 short-shank CdC Minimalistic Micro Midge immediately increased both the number of takes and successful hook-ups.

May and June 2019, was a time when the fish on my local rivers were often totally focused on aphids, completely ignoring the olives and mayflies; friends reported similarly from many other parts of the country. The big challenge for me was that the fish were mainly feeding in slow, shallow glides and the waters were desperately low and clear. Furthermore, on several windy days the river surface was littered with leafy debris (bits of leaf, leaf buds and sycamore flowers) which made seeing a size 24 to 30 imitation difficult and resulted in debris sticking to the hook if the fly wasn't taken virtually instantly (before any drag set in).

I've said it before and I'll say it again: accurate casting and good presentation are critical if success is to be achieved when fishing with tiny flies. Fish will usually not move any significant distance when feeding on tiny organisms as it's just not energy-efficient. Aphids resting on or trapped in the surface-film dead-drift, so any imitation must not suffer from even the slightest micro-drag if it is to look natural. Whilst trout will sometimes take an imitation as it starts to drag, grayling will normally reject a fly with even the slightest unnatural movement. To achieve a perfectly drag-free drift is very difficult and repeated attempts may be necessary to achieve success. The following will improve the angler's chance of achieving the perfect drift:

- Use long flexible (light) tippet (I use at least 5 ft of 0.09 mm copolymer).
- Tie your fly into a loop knot (Rapala Knot, Fordyce Loop or Perfection Loop) to give it free movement from the relatively stiff tippet.
- Use a flexible tapered leader (I use 7 ft of copolymer tapering from 0.43 mm to 0.20 mm diameter to which I attach my tippet; furled leaders are even more flexible).
- Use as light/thin/flexible a fly-line as possible (I usually use a Micro Nymph, zero-weight or a one-weight Micro Thin delicate presentation line with a 12 ft long front taper down to 0.55 mm diameter). You could consider using a silk line as they are far more flexible than plastic coated lines, however, with long rods they have a habit of wrapping around the rod tip, as do long furled leaders, and this can be a nuisance when wading.
- Use a suitable slack-line cast so that there is some slack in the line, particularly at the tippet end. You don't want a perfectly straight line between rod tip and fly as this will allow the instant onset of drag. The Italian Style slowed-down angular cast is perfect for putting slack into the leader and tippet whilst keeping the main line off any rogue currents.
- If possible cast across and slightly downstream with a dump/slack-line cast and an upstream reach, then track the rod tip downstream at the same pace as the current. Using a long rod will help with this.

The above things will reduce the effects of rogue currents pulling and pushing on the line and the last one will also ensure that the first thing the fish sees is the fly and not the line.

What about fly-patterns and hooks? Firstly, as mentioned earlier, there are times when size is critical. The more intense the rise, when aphids are super-abundant, the more important it is to have a really small fly. I keep reading about size 18 and 20 hooks used for aphid patterns but, as you'll see

Aphids from a grayling throat sample (photo by Stuart Crofts)

from Stuart Crofts' photo (see above) of a grayling's throat contents, aphids are only about 3 mm long and a size 30 short shank hook is more suitable for tying life-size imitations. There are very few really small hooks available to the fly-tyer and some are in my opinion not strong enough, whilst others have eyes that are far too small. My favourite hooks are Tiemco 2488s (which need the micro-barb flattening and appear now to be only made down to size 26) and Gamakatsu C12-BM (barbless and with the advantage of having a big eye). Other small hooks available in the UK are the Daiichi 1110 and Orvis Big Eye dry-fly hooks, which are identical and are made down to size 26 (the same length as a size 24 Tiemco 2488): their big eye is an advantage but the gape is a bit narrow for my liking and the barbs need to be flattened.

My pattern for aphids and midges is very simple. I usually tie my variant

An autumn grayling that fell to a size 30 CdC fly

A wild brown trout that fell for a size 24 IOBO Humpy, when the only surface flies were aphids

of Jack Tucker's deadly pattern the CdC IOBO (It Oughta Be Outlawed) Humpy in size 24. Below size 24 I tie my own Minimalistic Micro Midge, which is just the tip of a CdC feather tied facing over the hook eye. I generally tie these flies with tan 8/0 thread and natural greyish/tan mallard CdC. To aid visibility,

Size 30 IOBO Humpy against a mm scale, the size of a real aphid! (Gamakatsu C12-BM hook)

if I'm fishing against a light background, I treat the CdC with a thin coating of Roman Moser Miracle Float gel, whilst if the background is dark I apply white fumed silica powder. As you'll see from the throat contents photo (p 187) aphids come in a range of colours and flies tied with orange, yellow or even pink CdC work equally well if you need to improve their visibility. When accurately casting at relatively short range, I find that I have no problem seeing these miniscule flies (fishing at distances over 30 ft becomes counterproductive due to the reduced casting accuracy and the reduced hooking rate).

BEETLES

Summer is beetle time! It was in the late 1960s that I first came across a beetle imitation being used for trout. Eric Horsfall Turner, who fished the Yorkshire Derwent near to Scarborough, wrote in his book, *Angler's Cavalcade*, that he had stopped using his wet beetle imitation because it made catching trout too easy. As shown in the table below, beetles were a major part of the diet of the Derwent trout in the late 1990s when I still killed an occasional fish (I now fish totally catch-and-release except for any stocked rainbows, which I consider should never be put into a UK river).

Italian grayling that fell for a black beetle (photo by Stephen Donohue)

Diet of Yorkshire Derwent trout

FOOD ITEM	Numerical % of diet
black gnats	28
smuts/midges	21
beetles	17
olive nymphs	7
others	27

Eric's Beetle was a simple hackled wet-fly with a black hen's hackle, yellow wool underbody (left visible as a tag) and an over-body of peacock herl. I too found it to be very effective in my early days of flyfishing. Eric's Beetle has all the key features of an aquatic/water beetle with an air bubble held at its rear end. However, terrestrial beetles make up the vast majority of beetles that I have found in trout stomach contents, and nowadays I use a floating, foam beetle imitation which has over the years morphed into its simplest form, the Flip Flop Scarab Noire. I have also found this fly in its smaller sizes to be effective for grayling in Sweden and Italy, but have not as yet tried it for UK grayling.

Tying an Eric's Beetle

Hook Size 16 to 12 wet fly
Thread Black 6/0 or 8/0
Underbody Pale yellow wool (leave a little projecting at the tail end)
Overbody Peacock herl
Hackle Black hen

Tying a Flip Flop Scarab Noire

Hook Size 18 to 12 Partridge SLD, SLD 2, or similar
Thread Black 8/0 or 6/0
Underbody Dubbed Peacock Ice Dub or similar
Overbody and head 2 mm thick black sealed cell foam tied in just in front of the dubbed body
Legs 2 strands of single-knotted peacock herl
Sighter Pink poly-yarn

A liberal application of low viscosity Super Glue around the point where the foam is attached will prevent the foam rotating around the shank.

I tend to fish this pattern when there is no obvious hatch or fall of insects and my favoured places to fish it are where there is a heavy tree canopy (particularly on windy days) and along the margins of overhanging bankside vegetation. It is particularly effective when given frequent tiny twitches to simulate the struggles of a drowning beetle, which can induce incredibly aggressive takes. I find the best way of generating these tiny vibrations is with a long Tenkara rod and a super-light level Tenkara line, plus tippet about the same length as the rod. This facilitates a very direct contact between rod tip and fly such that all that is required is tapping of the rod butt with the forefinger to generate the required subtle movements. If the expected fish are too big for Tenkara then a long, light-line conventional rod with a French Leader/Micro Nymph line set-up or a one-weight Micro Thin line is the next best thing.

BIG MAYFLIES

Mayfly nymph

E danica *female dun*

What else could I talk about in May than the UK's two most common big mayflies, *Ephemera danica* and *Ephemera vulgata*? At the end of May and in early June, on many UK rivers and some lakes, anglers can look forward to the so-called "duffers' fortnight" when the nymphs transpose into adults. I say so-called because all too often, as I'll explain later, it can be a disappointment.

SOME THOUGHTS ON ENTOMOLOGY

E danica female spinner

Extended chenille-bodied Mayfly

However, if you hit conditions right there can be a bonanza of suicidal fish all too eager to engulf your big dry-flies.

E danica is the most frequent mayfly in trout waters as its nymphs prefer gravelly silt within which they tunnel, in most waters spending two years developing. *E vulgata* nymphs prefer the muddy silt of sluggish rivers and lakes. The duns are so similar as to be indistinguishable to most folks, whereas the spinners of *E vulgata* are a bit darker than those of *E danica*. The main time of emergence is generally during mid- to late-afternoon, whilst egg laying and spinner fall are evening events. As a result, if I intend fishing the mayfly I don't bother getting to the river till about 2 pm.

I rarely fish the Mayfly Nymph although it can be very effective fished sink and draw in the sluggish parts of the river prior to a hatch. However, I always have some weighted and unweighted Richard Walker Mayfly Nymphs in my box (just in case).

A big, light-coloured Klinkhåmer makes an effective emerger mayfly pattern. Despite several well-known flyfishers insisting that they need patterns to cover all stages of the mayfly's life I really only feel that I

Variant on Richard Walker's Mayfly Nymph

need one, which is a simple hackled version with an extended chenille body tied as follows:

Tying a chenille-bodied Mayfly

Hook	Size 12 or 14 Tiemco 206 BL (or similar short shank, wide gape dry-fly)
Thread	8/0 Tan, brown or orange
Tails	3 or 4 cock pheasant tail fibres
Abdomen	Andre Brun micro-chenille in tan or light olive
Thorax	Mix of brown and orange dubbing (under the hackle)
Hackle	1 olive and 1 grizzle cock (wound through each other and clipped in a V underneath)

This pattern works as both dun and spinner (for me). On the rare occasion that I've forgotten my mayfly pattern, I've found a Daddy to be equally effective since it has most of the same triggers (fish are far more stupid than we give them credit for!).

What is probably more important than the precise fly-pattern is the way it is fished. Whilst dead-drift usually works, the application of life-like movement can sometimes be more effective. The duns often skitter across the surface after emergence, trying to lift off. The application of similar movement to a dun pattern can result in explosive takes. On the other hand, spinners are best just twitched at intervals as they dead-drift. Tenkara with 5x tippet (the thickest recommended for Tenkara rods) is ideal for application of these subtle movements as long as the fish aren't too big and the fishing is close range. Whatever gear you use, don't go lighter than 5x tippet (4x or even 3x is probably better, particularly if the fish are big). To turn over these big flies effectively I use a shorter leader plus tippet than usual, about 12 ft with a long butt section of about 0.55 mm and tippet of about 0.15 to 0.20 mm.

Earlier on I referred to duffers' fortnight, but it is not always that easy. Quite often, particularly in the mornings or late in the hatch period, I find the trout ignoring the big mayflies and feeding on much smaller fare: black gnats, midges, small olives etc. So it pays to be observant and look carefully at what the fish are actually taking rather than what you want them to be taking or what you think they should be taking. A size 20 Shuttlecock or IOBO Humpy has accounted for a lot of the trout that I've caught during duffers' fortnight.

Thinking of small flies that can tempt trout away from the obvious food choice, such as big juicy mayflies, there is the case of the *Agapetus* caddis pupa mentioned elsewhere in this book.

ANTS

I am a great believer in keeping things simple when flyfishing and when fishing the dry-fly most of my fish come to four very basic patterns; a variant of Jack Tucker's CdC IOBO Humpy, a simple CdC Shuttlecock, Marjan Fratnick's F Fly and a basic Elk Hair Caddis tied with no hackle. However, there are some situations where these flies are not the ideal choice so I do have some more specialised flies in my box. On some New Zealand rivers during midsummer a size 18 or 20 Willow Grub can be an essential addition to the fly-box. I wouldn't be without some big Chernobyl Ants or Foam Beetles when fishing the high alpine streams of Austria and Italy. In late April/early May, I wouldn't be without a specific hawthorn fly pattern. Then there is the occasional day in late summer, in the UK and elsewhere, when flying ants emerge en masse. Also, on my local North Yorkshire Moors streams wood ants are prolific in the forests that border the upper reaches of many of the streams and on breezy days they frequently fall from the overhanging branches. Trout and grayling love ants. Maybe it is the sour taste of formic acid that they love, but whatever it is the fish can become preoccupied with them when there is a good fall of ants.

Austrian brook trout taken on a Foam Ant

I have two favourite patterns. The first is Stuart Crofts' F Ant, an F Fly variant that has a submerged body that helps to anchor the fly into the surface, and to resist micro-drag, whilst also making it appear vulnerable to the fish.

Tying a Stuart Crofts' F Ant

Hook   size 20 to 16 Grub
Thread   Black 8/0
Body   UV resin coated thread with a waist of red holographic tinsel
Wing and head   Natural mallard CdC

My second pattern is a simple Foam Ant of my own devising.

SOME THOUGHTS ON ENTOMOLOGY

Tying a Foam Ant

Hook Size 24 to 20 Short Shank (Tiemco 2488)
Thread Brown
Body Brown 2 mm thick sealed cell foam (trimmed to shape)
Hackle Rusty grizzle (trimmed top and bottom)
Wing White Tiemco Aerowing or similar

DANCE FLIES

Dance flies are two-winged flies (Order: Diptera, and members of the Family Empididae). There are many species, some of which swarm in vast numbers over water in search of their prey. It is their somewhat erratic, dancing, flight that gives them this common name. Their alternative common name is dagger flies, because they have a long, curved, sharp proboscis with which to feed on their prey (other flies), which they often take from the water surface. The males offer a captured prey item to the female during courtship. Sizes range from 5 to 15 mm (mostly around 7 mm long) and colour varies from yellow to black (mainly dark brown and black). They have a slim abdomen, fat thorax and small head.

Expect to see good numbers of them "dancing" in sunny spots that are sheltered from any strong wind any time during the summer. I find

A dance fly

Dance flies swarming in a sunny, sheltered spot

Trout that succumbed to a Black Gnat when feeding on dance flies

that a size 18 or 20 Black Gnat works as well as any other fly when trout are taking the occasional casualties that drift down below a hunting/mating swarm or those that are in the act of capturing a prey item from the river surface (I've even seen small trout jumping to take them in flight).

Tying a Black Gnat/Dance Fly

Hook   *Size 18 dry-fly*
Thread   *Black 8/0*
Body   *Fine black or dark brown synthetic dubbing*
Wing   *White poly-yarn*
Hackle   *Black cock clipped off at the bottom (and top clipped if you want a more visible wing whilst fishing)*

STONEFLIES

Stoneflies belong to a very primitive group of winged insects, the order Plecoptera. The UK has just over 30 species, with adults ranging from the slim willow and needle flies which have bodies from 4 to 11 mm long to relative monsters with bodies 24 mm long and a wing-span of 50 mm (2 in). They have four hard, shiny, strongly veined wings, the hind wings being broader than the fore wings. In some species the males have much reduced wings and are incapable of flight. When at rest, the wings are held flat across the back and extend well beyond the body. However, those of resting needle and willow flies, (*Leuctra* species), curl around the body, creating the typical needle shape. All have six sturdy legs, two antennae and two tails, which vary in their relative length from species to species. When tying imitations I ignore the antennae and tails, concentrating on the basic shape and wing length. In flight stoneflies are quite easy to identify since they look like fluttering biplanes.

The adults only live for a few days, but the nymphs generally spend a year crawling on the river bed (up to three years for some larger species), before emerging (generally at night) by crawling out of the water before exiting the nymphal exoskeleton. As a result, emergers are of no real interest to us. Whilst Steve Thornton and others tie some amazingly life-like Stonefly Nymph patterns I just stick to a simple Black Bead-head Hare's Ear or Pheasant Tail Nymph. Since I prefer the visual aspect of dry-fly fishing it is the adults that interest me most. Adults are particularly vulnerable when skittering over the surface or dipping during egg-laying and after.

Stonefly nymph

Few of the UK anglers I meet give dry stonefly fly patterns much thought despite the writings of the likes of Oliver Edwards, Paul Procter and Stuart Crofts on the subject. Stoneflies may never have the high profile in the UK that they do in parts of the USA. The spectacular hatches of huge salmon flies and slightly smaller golden stoneflies on rivers like Montana's Bitterroot are legendary, attracting even the biggest, virtually exclusively piscivorous, trout to the surface. Such frenzied feeding of big fish is not usually associated with UK stoneflies. Nevertheless, there are times, particularly in April, May and June, when adults of our larger species (members of the genera *Dinocras, Perla* and *Perlodes*) can be of importance to the British flyfisher on some of our spate rivers. Let me cite two times when imitations of these impressive insects have provided me with red letter days.

The first was a few years back during an early June trip to the Perthshire Tay at Aberfeldy. Evenings saw decent numbers of large brook spinners and sedges/caddis, to which the fish rose well, but during the bright, glaring sun of the day little insect life and virtually no risers were to be seen. Searching with nymphs proved ineffective and soon became tedious. Fortunately, I spotted an isolated large stonefly fluttering across the river only to disappear in an eruption of trout and spray. These large stoneflies, like big sedges and daddies, are big enough triggers to tempt fish, even when there is little vulnerable surface food.

Perlodes mortoni, orange striped stonefly, Cumbrian River Eamont

In response I attached a size 10 F Fly with a wing extending well beyond the hook bend and searched all the likely lies (current seams, under overhanging bankside trees and where turbulence showed the presence of submerged rocks). The fly was allowed to dead-drift interspersed with a few twitches and short pulls. The result? A pleasing number of quality trout launched themselves at my offering and that of my friend Steve Donohue.

The second instance was a fairly dull, breezy day in mid-May 2011, on the Cumbrian Eamont, with little insect life about; just an isolated hawthorn fly and a few black gnats. No fish were rising so I set up with a duo rig, size 12 Elk Hair Caddis and a size 18 Black Tungsten Bead-head Pheasant Tail Nymph. After fifteen minutes I had had no response. Then I saw a good, swirling rise 10 m above me. Covering it, I was rewarded with an equally vigorous rise to my Caddis. After a spirited fight a solid 35 cm grayling came to net. Whilst playing this fish I heard another splashy rise. Then I saw a large stonefly fluttering feebly across the river. I needed no further encouragement to remove the nymph and fish just the Large Caddis (which is also an excellent stonefly imitation). Another rise was covered and a 30 cm trout succumbed to the Caddis' charm. A similar sized fish was rising to black gnats and it fell to

3 lb 10 oz Eamont trout

a size 18 Black Gnat. I changed back to the size 12 Large Caddis and despite careful search-fishing the next twenty minutes was uneventful. Then tight against the far bank, just above the tail of the next pool, in mere centimetres of water, a good fish was popping up every few minutes. On the second cast my fly disappeared in a substantial swirl and all hell was let loose. He shot up the pool leaving a cascade of spray. After repeated strong runs he decided to head for the rapids at the pool tail, but his attempt was thwarted, leaving him wallowing right on the lip of the pool, massive tail waving aimlessly in thin air. His composure regained he shot back upstream, turned and headed, full pelt downstream into the rapids. I ran and stumbled after and finally managed to coax him to the net in the pool below; a cracking 3 lb 10 oz of wild, male brown trout. Several other fine fish followed on after this, some taking as I twitched/skated the fly, including one of 3 lb 1 oz. What a day!

When else can stonefly patterns be of use? On my local north-east Yorkshire rivers we see good numbers of small and medium sized stoneflies on sunny days in spring and again in autumn, with a sprinkling throughout the summer.

I use two main patterns; a two-winged CdC IOBO Humpy or Fluttering Stonefly to imitate the egg-laying adults and a CdC Spent Stonefly which lies cruciform in the surface film (my modification

Needle fly

and simplification of Oliver Edward's excellent pattern). Just occasionally, if I need to cast into a strong wind, I opt for a less air resistant, non-CdC pattern, a Wonder-wing Stone or a Hackle-less Elk Hair Caddis: the former, before my conversion to CdC, was my mainstay stonefly pattern. Its big drawbacks are that the wonder-wing soon gets shredded by trout teeth and unless the wing is absolutely horizontal the fly spins like a propeller when cast.

Grayling love small stoneflies and one of my most memorable sessions fishing for them was a September day on Slovenia's River Soča. Steve Donohue and I had been advised by the locals that it was little use fishing till 10 am, so for the previous ten days we'd taken their advice. We'd caught a fair number of good grayling and rainbows, plus an isolated small marbled trout, but we'd had to work for our fish as hatches of olives were sparse and only isolated stoneflies were about. However, on our last day we started early and in the hour between 9 am and 10 am, just as the sun got onto the bankside trees, an abundance of medium-sized stoneflies appeared, fluttering and egg-laying on the river, and fish started to take them. A dozen grayling around the 35 to 40 cm mark and a couple of 45 cm plus rainbows fell to our size 14 Two Feather IOBO Humpies. Then after 10 am things quietened down and only occasional fish were caught.

So, next time you're fishing a spate river keep your eye open for stoneflies and make sure you've got a few suitable patterns in your fly-box.

When tying dry stonefly patterns my main considerations are that they:

- Have the correct basic profile/shape.

- Are the correct size.

- Are approximately the correct colour (as I've said before, I'm not convinced that colour is particularly important in dry-fly design).

- Fish correctly on or in the surface film.

- Can be cast without spinning and twisting the leader/tippet.

- Are easy to tie and durable.

You'll note I've not been highly specific regarding materials and exact colours since I find a host of alternatives work equally effectively. Too many fly-tyers seem to fuss excessively about the minutiae of the patterns and not enough about their overall appearance and how they behave during fishing (and casting).

Tying a hackle-less Elk Hair Caddis/Stone

Hook *Fine wire dry-fly sizes 18 to 10*
Thread *Tan/Brown 8/0 or 6/0*
Body *Roped natural dark grey/brown CdC, dubbed hare's ear, or other brown/tan dubbing (I use fine dubbing for small flies and medium for larger ones)*
Underwing *(optional)* *Natural CdC feather tip or fine brown deer hair*
Wing *Pale tan or bleached elk, extending beyond the body (colour to aid visibility)*

SOME THOUGHTS ON ENTOMOLOGY

Tying an F Fly

Hook *Fine wire dry-fly sizes 18 to 10*
Thread *Brown 8/0*
Body *Roped natural dark grey/brown CdC, hare's ear or other brown/tan dubbing: just thread, or stripped peacock herl stem (coated with Super Glue, Bug Bond or varnish) for small sizes*
Wing *3 or 4 natural dark grey/brown CdC tips tied flat across the back, extending beyond the body*
Hackle/Legs *(optional) CdC fibres put into a split loop, which is spun and then wound as a hackle and trimmed underneath*

Tying a Yellow Sally Stonefly

Hook *Fine wire dry-fly size 16/14*
Thread *Yellow 8/0*
Body *Lime-yellow CdC (roped), wound lime-yellow Antron yarn or fine lime-yellow dubbing*
Wing *Bunch of lime-yellow Antron/poly-yarn or 3 or 4 lime-yellow CdC tips, extending beyond the body*
Hackle/Legs *(optional) Lime-yellow CdC fibres or cut Antron yarn fibres put into a split loop, spun, then wound as a hackle & trimmed underneath*

Tying a CdC Spent Stonefly

Hook	Fine wire dry-fly sizes 18 to 14
Thread	Tan/brown 8/0
Body	Stripped peacock herl stem (coated with Super Glue or Bug Bond for strength) or fine brown poly dubbing
Wings	4 natural, dark brown/grey CdC tips (2 tied pointing backwards and 2 forwards. Then positioned with figure-of-eight turns of dubbed thread and finally trimmed to shape)
Thorax	Fine brown poly dubbing or hare's ear figure-of-eighted around the wing bases
Tails and Antennae (optional)	2 moose hair fibres at tail and 2 at the head (though I don't bother with them)

Tying a double-feather IOBO Humpy (Fluttering Stone)

Hook	Fine wire dry-fly sizes 16 to 10
Thread	Tan/brown 8/0
Body	Thread (well-waxed to waterproof)
Back	Base of the 2 CdC feathers tied in for the wings
Wings	2 natural dark brown/grey CdC feather tips splayed out to about 90 degrees.
Tails	A few CdC fibres left trailing when the wings are pulled forward, over the back, during tying

SOME THOUGHTS ON ENTOMOLOGY

CADDIS FLIES

Cased caddis larvae

Hydropsyche *caseless caddis*

Rhyacophila *caseless caddis*

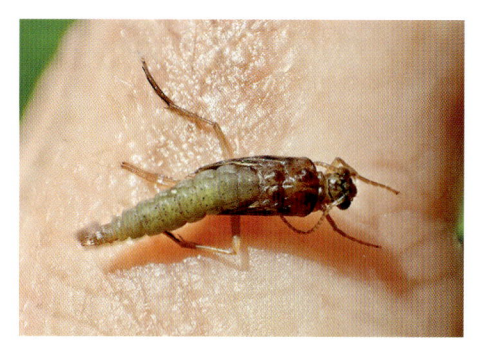

Rhyacophila *pharate adult/pupa*

Cinammon sedge, Limnephilus lunatus

Agapetus fuscipes

There are approximately 200 species of caddis fly or sedge in the UK. They are closely related to moths and the most obvious difference between an adult caddis fly and a moth is that the former have four hairy wings, whilst the latter have scales covering their wings. Caddis larvae are aquatic and caterpillar-like, and like caterpillars they can produce silken threads – with which most species build a protective case from pieces of vegetation, debris, sand or stones. However, some larvae are free-living, building nets of silken threads within which they live. They range from 3 mm long to about 3 cm. Prior to pupation the larva anchors itself to a firm substrate and metamorphosis takes place within a silken cocoon. When mature the pharate adult (what anglers call a pupa) bites its way out of the cocoon and swims to the surface where it either emerges and flies away, or in some cases, such as *Agapetus*, it swims to the bank where it finally transposes into the adult form. All three main stages are of interest to the flyfisher. Adults vary in size from tiny micro-caddis less than 5 mm long to large specimens of 3 cm.

Cased larvae are well imitated with a Peeping Caddis.

Tying a Peeping Caddis

Hook   Jig hook 16 to 10
Thread   8/0 tan
Body/case   Hare's ear dubbing (plus green glister optional)
Legs   Brown partridge hackle
Peeping Body and head   Singed green or yellow synthetic wool or chenille
Weight   Black tungsten bead

SOME THOUGHTS ON ENTOMOLOGY

Caseless caddis larvae are well imitated by Czech-style Nymphs.

Tying a *Hydropsyche* Czech Nymph

Hook Grub/Czech Nymph hook 16 to 10
Thread 8/0 tan
UnderBody Single layer of lead wire or foil
Body Hare's ear rear and brown squirrel front
Back Dark brown shell-back
Rear appendages *(optional)* partridge filoplume

Tying a *Rhyac* Czech Nymph

Hook Grub/Czech Nymph hook size 16 to 10
Thread 8/0 yellow
UnderBody Single layer of lead wire or foil
Body Green furry foam or dubbing rear and brown squirrel front
Back Grey or olive shellback

To imitate adult caddis I mainly use either a simple hackle-less Elk Hair Caddis or an F Fly.

Tying a hackle-less Elk Hair Caddis

Hook Dry-fly size 20 to 10
Thread 8/0 or 6/0 tan
Body Hare's ear or mask dubbing
Wing Bleached elk (optional brown deer or CdC underwing)

Tying a Hi-vis F Fly

Hook   *Dry-fly size 20 to 10*
Thread   *8/0 tan*
Body   *Roped CdC*
Wing   *3 to 4 CdC feather tips*
Hi-vis overwing *(optional)*   *Dyed CdC*
Legs *(optional)*   *CdC in split thread*

I find that the larval imitations are best fished dead-drift, whilst pupae/pharate adult and adult patterns are often best fished dead-drift and with frequent twitches or even more vigorous pulls to induce a take.

TIPULIDS/CRANEFLIES

There are 327 species of crane fly or daddy long legs in the UK and adults range from 7 mm long to over 4 cm, all with slim bodies, long legs and two wings. The grey-brown, maggot-like larvae live in moist habitats, both terrestrial and aquatic, where they feed on algae and organic detritus. I often see them in my kick samples of aquatic invertebrates.

Little or nothing hatching? Few fish rising? With declining populations of Ephemerids (upwing flies), this is an increasingly common scenario on many rivers. Even on my local Yorkshire Derwent, which still has healthy Ephemerid populations, there are times during May, June,

Aquatic Tipulid larva

July and August when hatches are sparse and surface activity minimal. It is then that terrestrials come into their own. On windy days, the windier the better, wooded sections of the river can provide a bonanza of dislodged beetles, wood ants and greenflies. Under these conditions the fish are usually opportunistic feeders, taking whatever fly is put over them. If it lands with a plop then so much the better. The choice of fly is yours; Foam Beetle, black Klinkhåmer, Sedge etc. The following stomach analysis from a Yorkshire Derwent trout is typical of such days in August:

Adult Tipulid

- 10 black gnats, 3 medium-sized black Diptera (bluebottle-type flies), 1 ichneumon fly, 61 wood ants, 5 black beetles.

On calm days it can be very different. Few terrestrials are blown onto the water; there is no hatch and the river looks dead. What can the dry-fly fisher do? Do we walk for miles searching for a riser? Do we go home? Or do we go to the pub to drown our sorrows? *No!* Now is the time to use our watercraft and call on Daddy for help. Some people use a sedge as their choice of "search-fly", but my usual choice is the Daddy-Long-Legs for trout (not for grayling since they seem reticent about taking them).

How do I fish my Daddy and why does he work so well? Many anglers will tell you that late summer is the Daddy season, but craneflies are about from April till September. The adults are all substantial enough to tempt a fish to the surface and their feeble struggles in the surface film advertise their presence. Trout detect these vibrations with their lateral line pressure receptors.

Although the fish don't see them often (other than during the late summer glut), they certainly know what they are and rise to them with gusto. I usually fish them dead-drift, but if this fails I give a short, sharp twitch or two. Takes to the twitched fly can be explosive so I step up to a 5 lb plus tippet (4x). I must admit that blind casting is not my favourite style of fishing, but searching with a dry-fly is the same as searching with a nymph. I look for the likely lies, where the current swings under trees, by roots or against steep banks. I also search the current seams/foam lanes and in front of and behind boulders and weed-beds, where there are steep drop offs or even where there are slight depressions in a shallow riffle. I never ignore the really "skinny" water, particularly in hot sunny conditions. The shallow riffles between pools are well-oxygenated, whilst the rippled surface provides cover for the fish. Last summer I had three nice wildies from a tiny 12 in deep pocket in a 6 in deep riffle.

As an entomologist I always try to fish appropriate imitative patterns, whether fishing wet or dry. The Daddy is one such pattern and I rather take him for granted. Stillwater flyfishers are well aware of the value of the Daddy. However, a few years ago I was reminded that some river anglers are not so familiar with his potential. It had been a baking hot day on the Yorkshire Derwent and I was having a slow evening, with just a sprinkling of small fish falling to my size 16 Paraloop Red Spinner. Not much was rising and there were only a few yellow mayflies, olives and spinners about. A change to the twitched Daddy immediately brought improved success, with more and bigger fish coming to the net. That evening a friend rang for some advice. He too had found the fishing very slow. I suggested he try a Daddy next time and since he had none, I tied him up a few, which I delivered early the following day. He kindly exchanged them for a bottle of Chablis. That evening he phoned: he'd had a great session with the Daddy and informed me that there were plenty more bottles of wine if I had more Daddies to spare.

Forgotten your box of Mayflies or maybe you've lost your last Mayfly on an overhanging branch? It's an afternoon in late May or early June and the trout

Caught on a Daddy

are going mad on emerging mayfly duns. Don't worry! I've done it a few times myself. I've yet to find a trout feeding on mayflies which won't take a Daddy. They provide the same basic triggers. In fact, early in a mayfly hatch, when the trout are really slashing at the mayflies but often missing them, I find I have far fewer missed takes if I use a Daddy.

Midsummer and you're on a stillwater… The trout are erupting after damsel flies skimming the surface. You've no adult damsel patterns! No worries; call on Daddy yet again. A Daddy skated across the surface works fine. Never mind that the damsels are blue and your Daddy is brown; the trout don't mind so why should you. Do, however, use at least 8 lb tippet. This can be exciting stuff with browns and rainbows bow-waving after your fly. Takes can be vicious.

So, don't forget to enlist the help of your Daddy next time risers are few and far between, damsels are on the menu, or you've not got your Mayflies. He'll be a real help.

How to tie Daddy? One good pattern is a modification of the late, great, Richard Walker's pattern. He found that legs trailing backwards were not only easier to tie than splayed ones, but that they were more effective.

I feel too many people get overly concerned with the fine detail of fly dressings and materials used. I am much more concerned with the overall impression of the fly and how it fishes/sits in/on the water. Don't get me wrong… Sometimes the materials used do affect how the fly looks and fishes, but there may be a dozen or more ways to tie the same fly effectively. The following is my method for the Daddy, chosen because it is effective, durable, easy and quick to tie, in that order of importance.

Tying an extended chenille-bodied Daddy

Hook	14 or 12 short shank Tiemco 2488 or 206BL
Body	Extended body of brown micro-chenille
Hackle	Grizzle generic cock trimmed underneath
Legs	8 single knotted cock pheasant tail fibres (4 on each side)

Tipulid larvae are well imitated by Frank Sawyer's Killer Bug.

Tying a Killer Bug

Hook	Sizes 14 to 10 straight shank
Tying Thread	Copper wire
Body	1 strand of Chadwick's 477 wool (or similar)

5

SOME THOUGHTS ON CONSERVATION AND FISHERY MANAGEMENT

A PRECIOUS RESOURCE

Our trout and grayling are a valuable resource (particularly the wild ones) yet it seems to me that too many flyfishers and club officials treat them with little respect. They treat them as an exploitable resource, or a saleable commodity and nothing more. At one club AGM, when the stocking policy was being discussed, a member said, "Why are we worried about the grayling stocks? We are running a trout fishery," whilst another said, "Our fishery is a put-and-take water, run so that our members can catch fish and we shouldn't be concerned about the wild fish." Yet another said, "Our river doesn't produce wild fish over eight inches..." as a justification for stocking a small stream with large numbers of 1½ to 3 lb brown trout and rainbows. All I can say is that friends and I catch plenty of wild fish over 10 in on the water in question, with isolated wildies to 14 in.

The contentious issue of stocking is a major concern of mine. I am convinced that the heavy stocking of fisheries capable of sustaining wild stocks of trout and grayling is detrimental to the recruitment and survival of the wild fish. I've watched big, newly stocked brown trout in a local beck herding the grayling fry just like in the programmes we see on the TV where bait balls of sardines are annihilated by sharks, dolphins etc. Moreover, on numerous occasions I, and my friends, have had large stockies (particularly rainbows) attack and kill small grayling and trout whilst we've been playing them. I am fairly sure that the relatively low grayling numbers presently found in the aforementioned stream reflect the club's stocking policy. Although it is impossible to obtain statistically significant proof of this, the evidence I have accumulated is very suggestive thereof. My catch rate on the unstocked parts of this river is nearly three times that on the stocked parts. It seems too much of a coincidence that immediately after two years when smaller (25 to 30 cm) stockies were put into the river four things happened:

1. Grayling numbers increased dramatically.
2. The numbers of big grayling (35 cm plus) increased dramatically.
3. The minnow population (usually very low) increased dramatically.
4. Small chub (under 15 cm) appeared for the first time in decades.

Since returning to a policy of stocking with big browns and rainbows (35 to 40 cm plus) the grayling and minnow populations have collapsed and no more small chub have been seen. Sadly, many club members want easily caught, big fish, judging their success by the number and size of fish they catch and not by the challenges they have overcome to catch them. I've caught stockie rainbows of well over 10 lb (from stillwaters), but feel little pride at their capture since I know they were put into the water at that size. I will freely confess that I like catching big fish and two of my most memorable catches have been of a 4 lb wild brown from a tiny Yorkshire limestone brook and a 4 lb 12 oz wild brown from the Yorkshire Rye. Nevertheless, I don't need large numbers or big fish to have a great day. In late March 2009 I had a fabulous day on the Cumbrian Eden. There had been a hard frost and blazing sun was shining on a very low, gin-clear river. A hatch of large dark olives started to lift off just before noon. With the warm sun they weren't lingering long on the surface. Seeing no risers, I fruitlessly searched likely seams and bubble lines at a pool head with a duo rig. I soon tired of this, so wandered downstream to a series of riffles where I found a couple of risers. Targeting one I eased my way across the river to a spot where I thought I could achieve a drag free drift. *Wrong!* The flows were awkward and an upstream cast along the seam edge resulted in virtually instant drag. On the third drift the fish came short just as drag was starting and immediately after I had another take as I was lifting off, just prior to drag setting in. Chance blown? After a brief wait it started to rise again. A move of position to where I could cast down and across, with a slack-line plus a reach-cast, followed by tracking with the rod, reduced the drag problem and on the fifth cast, bingo, a lively little 27 cm trout was on. I photographed it underwater with my new waterproof digital camera (a very fish-friendly bit of kit). Another fish was rising in the fast flow halfway up the same riffle. It took my CdC Gasparin Dun first cast and exploded into the air twice before shedding the hook. I consoled myself with the fact that at least I'd tempted it to take my fly. I missed another take soon after. Isolated March browns started to appear and in the next riffle I heard, rather than saw, a slashing rise. It had to be to a March brown, so I changed to a size 14 Oliver Edwards' March Brown. Second drift a 32 cm brownie launched itself at my fly, taking to the air as it did. By 2pm the hatch had stopped. I'd only caught two relatively small fish, but I was well pleased. I'd seen buzzards, dippers, wagtails, field voles, hares and some great scenery on a glorious day. What more could one ask for? Who wants loads of easy stew-fed stockies? *Not me!*

Let's get back to the point. Other potential problems associated with stocking are the possible introduction of disease. A few years back the transfer of stocked fish in parts of Yorkshire was temporarily stopped due to an outbreak of VHS (viral haemorrhagic septicaemia) on the Nidd, linked to a trout farm. Despite all precautions, high density rearing of fish provides good conditions for the spread of disease.

Another concern of mine is the physical damage done to fish by careless handling. On waters where catch-and-release is the normal practice many anglers would be amazed at how often individual fish are recaptured.

Carp anglers have long been aware of this, to the extent of naming certain recognisable fish. Their use of barbless hooks, soft mesh nets and unhooking mats attest to the concern they have for their quarry's welfare. Few game fish have such distinctive markings enabling sure identification. However, there was one big grayling in Driffield West Beck that did have a recognisable spot pattern and which I caught four times in eighteen months. Careless handling can lead to fungal infection and death. I think barbless or debarbed hooks should be made mandatory on all fisheries where catch-and-release is permitted. Should anglers have to pass a written test before being permitted to buy a fishing licence? Maybe. I see many who seem disturbingly unaware of how fish should be handled. I saw one guy holding fish in a dry towel whilst unhooking them. His reason? To stop them slipping out of his hands. He was unaware that this would remove the protective slime from the fish, leaving them vulnerable to infection. Others keep a fish out of the water for ages whilst they unhook, weigh and photograph their prize; after which they fail to nurse the fish in the water till fully recovered before release. As a result, the fish turns belly up and dies. Some stand whilst posing for a photograph, only to inadvertently drop the fish from a great height onto the ground; far better to kneel with the fish at ground level, or even better have a photo taken whilst releasing the fish in the water. Few have the camera ready before the fish is removed from the water in order to reduce any delay in returning the fish. A good rule is, "If in doubt miss the photo out." Don't forget to handle fish with wet hands, again to avoid removal of protective slime. I used to use a Ketchum-style release tool, but now have mixed feelings about its use; I found I had to play fish to a standstill before they would remain still enough to be easily released and even with barbless hooks, if unhooking was not instantaneous, some fish would thrash about causing the hook to tear out of the mouth. I now either bring small fish to hand or use a fine, soft mesh net to handle bigger fish. Recently, floating nets have become available, thanks to Glen Pointon, and for the wading angler they are a godsend since the fish do

Glen Pointon Floating Net

not need to be removed from the water, even for unhooking, and exhausted fish can be left to recover in the net.

A third worry of mine is "Fishmonger Syndrome" which a few anglers seem to suffer from. This is fine on waters stocked with takeable-sized fish since, on all but the most productive of waters, stockies have a limited survival rate. However, on wild fisheries the removal of significant numbers of the larger wild fish will have a detrimental effect on the gene pool, removing those beneficial genes that confer fast growth rate, leading to a race of stunted trout. I am pleased to say that on some enlightened fisheries where supplementary stocking is used, the stockies are marked with a spot of dye on the belly or clipped fins, with catch-and-release of wild fish (trout and grayling) being mandatory. On some wild fisheries such as the upper Yorkshire Don a slot limit is imposed where only 10 to 12 in (25 to 30 cm) fish may be killed. A few years back, on a small north-east Yorkshire stream, which holds only a

Plenty of large woody debris and plenty of fish in Thornton Beck!

moderate head of grayling, my friend Steve saw a member with a couple of dead 35 cm plus grayling. These were the prime breeding stock needed to propagate the next generation of this short-lived species (a maximum life span of less than six years in many UK rivers). If a significant proportion of the 90-plus members of the club removed big grayling from this tiny stream the population would be decimated.

Finally, I come to overzealous "gardening" of rivers and riverbanks. Some clubs, and particularly their work parties, seem to be hell-bent on the removal of every shred of bankside vegetation or overhanging tree that might snag the fly of an unwary angler. Every debris dam or fallen tree in the water must be removed. The result? Less cover for the fish, which move out of the stretch or more easily fall prey to predators: less cover for the bank-fisher hence fewer fish caught: less habitat diversity for both terrestrial and aquatic invertebrates, so less food for the fish. Everybody loses! The two most heavily populated streams in my area are both unmanaged, overgrown waters full of fallen trees, smaller woody debris and alder roots. Thankfully, most club members don't want to fish them. As a result they are neglected which suits me and the fish fine.

We really must take care of our fish and fisheries. As individuals we are only going to exploit them for a very short time. We are custodians of a precious, finite resource. What will we leave for the next generation? A wasteland of ruined, stockie-filled fisheries, or wonderful streams teaming with wild life and with a sufficiency of challenging wild fish? The choice is ours.

CONSERVATION GROUPS (WILD TROUT TRUST, WILDFISH CONSERVATION, RIVERS TRUSTS, RIVERFLY PARTNERSHIP)

I am a member of the Angling Trust, a keen supporter of the Wild Trout Trust (WTT) and Salmon and Trout Conservation (now called Wildfish Conservation), a trustee of the East Yorkshire Rivers Trust and both a sampler and tutor for the Riverfly Partnership. Only by giving our support to these conservation groups can we hope to protect those waters and fish species that are in good health and aid the recovery of those that are in decline.

Over my 50-plus years as an angler I have watched the insidious decline of many of the waters that I have fished. The huge shoals of quality grayling that used to be found in every part of my local Driffield Beck have all but disappeared due to abstraction, siltation, diffuse pollution and cormorant predation. Oxfolds and Costa Beck, near Pickering in North Yorkshire, went from being the local club's primary fishery, famous throughout the UK for its abundant big grayling and huge wild trout, to a stream devoid of all but a few escapee trout from the local trout farm and it is only just now showing some signs of recovery after over fifteen years of battle by the local club and Fish Legal to resolve the problems. I hear similar stories from all over the UK.

An Oxfolds/Costa Beck grayling before the beck was destroyed

The sewage outfall on Costa Beck, which was still as bad in 2019 as 2011

A grayling from a once dead industrial Yorkshire river

A small glimmer of hope is the amazing recovery of the industrial rivers in West Yorkshire and Lancashire where grayling and trout proliferate thanks to the decline of some polluting industries and the incredibly hard work of groups such as SPRITE on the Sheffield Don and the work of individuals like Stuart Crofts, also on the Don. Nature has an incredible capacity for recovery given half a chance.

My own local Pickering Beck has benefited from the work and

Pickering Beck's Duchy Water; a Wild Trout Trust training day, introducing woody debris

Protection from erosion and ingress of silt on Pickering Beck

advice from the Wild Trout Trust and the Pickering Fishery Association gained a WTT Award for the follow-up work done by club members, with the help of the East Yorkshire Rivers Trust, to improve the habitat on the upper reaches of the beck.

The Riverfly Partnership is a body based at the Freshwater Biological Association on the shores of Lake Windermere, Cumbria. The work is carried out by trained volunteers who do kick sampling (usually monthly) on their local rivers and streams to monitor the health of the invertebrate populations. Samplers carry out a three-minute kick sample and a one-minute search of rocks, after which they estimate the numbers of aquatic invertebrates belonging to eight indicator groups (cased caddis larvae, caseless caddis larvae, *Baetis* nymphs, blue-winged olive nymphs, big mayfly nymphs, Heptageneid nymphs, stonefly nymphs and *Gammarus*/shrimps). The data is imported into a national database and any problems – as indicated by an unexpected change in invertebrate numbers and diversity – can be dealt with immediately by the Environment Agency.

A Riverfly Partnership training day, Yorkshire River Rye

Investigating a kick sample

Nick Measham, chief executive officer of Wildfish Conservation (Salmon and Trout Conservation), playing a grayling on the River Itchen

More in-depth aquatic invertebrate studies have been carried out as a small part of the work of the Salmon and Trout Conservation group. They have mainly been carried out on the southern chalk streams to date and have shown a very worrying picture of the state of many of these precious and supposedly protected waters. Abstraction, siltation, diffuse pollution (particularly of phosphates) have taken their toll, particularly impacting on the once super-abundant blue winged olives.

I would urge every angler to support these conservation bodies, since without them I fear our rivers and lakes would be in a far worse state even than they are now and would continue to decline as habitats not just for the fish but all the other wildlife that depends on clean, healthy waters.

Signs like this can be found at many river access points in New Zealand and anglers visiting the back country have to take disinfectant kits with them

BIOSECURITY

There are an increasing number of alien species invading our lakes and rivers. Many of them have been shown to be causing serious damage to our indigenous flora and fauna, including the fish that we anglers so cherish. Unfortunately, many UK anglers appear to have little regard to the need for biosecurity measures, however, any angler visiting New Zealand will be well-aware of how serious the authorities there are about it.

Let's first of all consider some species that impact directly or indirectly on our fishing:

- The **Killer Shrimp** (*Dikerogammarus villosus*), a Ponto-Caspian invader from Eastern Europe. In 2010 it was discovered in Grafham Water, Cardiff Bay and Eglwys Nunydd Reservoir in Wales, then in 2012 in the Norfolk Broads and in 2015 at Pitsford Reservoir. It is a serious predator of other invertebrates, fish eggs and very young fish.

- The **Demon Shrimp** (*Dikerogammarus haemobaphes*) is another Ponto-Caspian invader that was first discovered in 2012 in the River Severn at Tewkesbury and which has spread widely throughout the canals and rivers of England. They prey on other Gammarids and aquatic insects.

- The **Tiger Shrimp** (*Gammarus tigrinus*) was first seen in the UK in 1931 and has spread widely throughout the UK, including my local Driffield Beck. It does not appear to be as damaging to aquatic ecosystems as the larger *Dikerogammarus* species.

Gammarus tigrinus *from Driffield Beck*

- The **Signal Crayfish** (*Pacifastacus leniusculus*) was introduced to English fish farms in 1975. It is now widespread throughout England, Wales and Scotland. It spreads **Crayfish Plague** (*Aphanomyces astaci*), a fungus that attacks and kills our native white-clawed crayfish (*Austropotamobius pallipes*). Furthermore, it and other non-native crayfish species are a serious predatory threat to our other native aquatic invertebrates, especially slow and static caddis larvae and pupae, and to fish eggs.

- **Bloody-red Mysid** (*Hemimysis anomala*) is another Ponto-Caspian shrimp-like crustacean species first recorded in the UK in 2004 on the River Trent at the international water sports centre and also found in Rutland Water and some other reservoirs in England, also in Eire's Lough Derg and the River Shannon in 2008. They breed very rapidly, can tolerate wide ranges of salinity and predate heavily on small zooplankton such as *Daphnia* that are a key component of aquatic food chains.

Mink, Driffield Beck   *Water vole, Driffield Beck*

- **Mink** (*Neovison vison*), a North American invader, escaped or was released by animal welfare activists from UK mink farms in the 1960s through until the 1990s. They are serious predators of most riverine wildlife including fish. Mink have devastated water vole populations.

- **Himalayan balsam** (*Impatiens glandulifera*), a garden escapee from the Kashmir, it outcompetes other river-bank flora and dies back in the autumn leaving bare banks that are easily eroded.

- **Japanese knotweed** (*Fallopia japonica*) was introduced to gardens from Eastern Asia in the mid-1800s and had escaped to the wild by the late 1800s. It is very invasive and highly damaging to flood defences.

- **Giant hogweed** (*Heracleum mantegazzianum*) a native of Russia, has highly damaging sap that, when it gets onto skin and is exposed to the sun, can cause serious blistering.

Possible invaders that might have a serious impact:

- **Salmon fluke** (*Gyrodactylus salaris*) a parasite that affects salmon, trout and grayling. It has virtually wiped out salmon in a number of Norwegian rivers and is found in a number of other European countries. Its impact, should it get into our UK rivers, could be devastating.

In addition to these invaders there are a number of diseases that can easily be spread by our careless actions. These include:

- **Viral hemorrhagic septicemia (VHS)** a very contagious, deadly disease that affects a wide range of fish species. It caused fish deaths on the River Nidd in 2006 that led to restrictions in transfer of stocked trout in the area.

- **Koi herpes virus** affects all varieties of common and ornamental carp, resulting in a high mortality rate. Many flyfishers are now targeting carp, risking the transfer of virus between waters.

How can we reduce the risk of spreading these invasive species and diseases to areas where they are at present absent? We need strict biosecurity when we move from one water to another. All the required information is available at the following websites: http://www.nonnativespecies.org/sitemap and http://www.nonnativespecies.org/checkcleandry/biosecurity-for-anglers

However, the simplest ways to avoid transfer of unwanted pests and diseases are as follows:

1. Thoroughly clean all equipment (waders, wading boots, landing nets, etc.). Thoroughly dry these items (they need to be dry for 48 hours) or soak in very hot tap water (60°C) for 15 minutes).
2. If possible avoid the use of felt soles on wading boots or have several pairs of boots, each of which is only used on one water.
3. Rinsing in Virkon S disinfectant will kill a wide range of viruses, bacteria and fungi (but not invasive invertebrates if it is the only measure that is used). Many fisheries have net- and boot-dipping facilities that should be used before and after fishing.
4. When fishing rivers and moving upstream check that the lower parts of your fishery do not hold invasive species that have not reached the upper parts. When I carry out my monthly river fly invertebrate kick sampling I always start at the upstream sites first.

IN CONCLUSION

I hope readers of this book have found it enjoyable and informative. Nearly all that I have learned about flyfishing has been thanks to the writings and generosity of others. Sharing is one of the most rewarding aspects of fishing; sharing ideas; sharing experiences and sharing laughter.

If like me you have a thirst for further knowledge and insight into how trout behave I can thoroughly recommend Peter Hayes and Don Stazicker's ebook *Trout and Flies: Getting Closer* which, thanks to the use of superb quality still and video photography, gives an in-depth insight into how trout feed and how we should approach their capture. They debunk many long-held opinions, some of which have become enshrined in flyfishing lore. They also share many innovative fly patterns that their studies have helped them design.

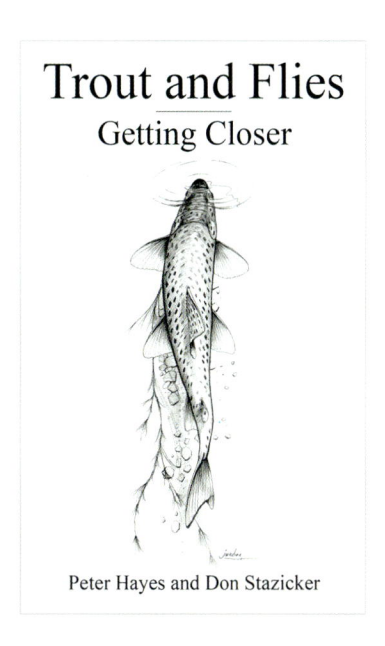

The monetary profits from this book will be split 50:50 between the Wild Trout Trust and Wildfish/Salmon and Trout Conservation.

A LIST OF BOOKS
On flyfishing and fishing flies published by Coch-y-Bonddu Books

GRAYLING ON THE FLY
John Roberts

FLY FISHING OUTSIDE THE BOX
Peter Hayes

GRAYLING FLIES
Steve Skuce

DRY-FLY FISHING FOR GRAYLING
Vincenzo Penteriani

GRAYLING FISHING
William Carter Platts

BROOK AND RIVER TROUTING
H H Edmonds and N N Lee

THE NORTH COUNTRY FLY
Robert L Smith

PLU STINIOG:
TROUT FLIES FOR NORTH WALES
Emrys Evans

THE FORGOTTEN FLIES
OF ROGER WOOLLEY
John N Watson

WILD LAKES OF WALES:
AN ANGLER'S GUIDE
Ceri Thomas and Alan Parfitt

REFLECTIONS ON THE LOCH
Stan Headley

FRENCH FISHING FLIES
Jean-Paul Pequegnot

SALMON FLIES: PAST & PRESENT
Henk van Bork

THE ESSENTIAL KELSON
Compiled by Terry Griffiths

FARLOWS SALMON FLIES
Martin Lanigan O'Keeffe

HARDY'S SALMON FLIES
Martin Lanigan O'Keeffe

SALTWATER FLYFISHING:
BRITAIN & NORTHERN EUROPE
Paul Morgan and friends

MULLET ON THE FLY
Colin MacLeoed

FLYFISHING THE WELSH BORDERLANDS
Roger S D Smith

Additionally, we produce beautiful editions of classic flyfishing books by Francis, Pritt, Walbran, Halford, Skues and many others in our Flyfisher's Classic Library series.
All can be seen at www.anglebooks.com